T0019804

"Patrick Schreiner's book *The Ascension of Christ* is an excellent treatment of an important but often overlooked aspect of Christ's work. In very short space, Schreiner provides a remarkably comprehensive and clear analysis of the ascension. He writes with humor, warmth, and theological precision. This book is without doubt one of the best works that has been written on the ascension."

—**Peter Orr**, lecturer,
Moore Theological College, Sydney, Australia

"Noting that Christ's ascension is an important but neglected area of theology, Schreiner provides an insightful, pithy, and accessible introduction to the topic, particularly demonstrating its significance for Christ's threefold office of prophet, priest, and king. Readers will find this book to be well-organized, brief yet thorough, biblically deep (especially in its use of the Old Testament), and theologically precise. This book is a wonderful one-stop shop for learning about the significance of Christ's ascension for theology and for the church's practice."

—**Gavin Ortlund**, senior pastor,
First Baptist Church of Ojai, California

"Patrick Schreiner tells how, beginning from the book of Acts, he started looking around and soon came to see the ascension everywhere. That is exactly how this doctrine is: easy enough to overlook, but astonishing in its scope and significance as soon as you start paying attention. This book is a great guide to the importance of Jesus' ascension and an invitation to start seeing it everywhere."

—**Fred Sanders**, Torrey Honors Institute,
Biola University

"With Christians so focused on the death and resurrection of Jesus (and rightly so), we sometimes ignore or neglect what happened after that, much to our loss. Schreiner beautifully and brilliantly guides us through the completion of Christ's work in his ascension and session at the Father's right hand. Christ's work as our prophet, priest and king deserves honor and devotion in every aspect, including his post-resurrection ministry. If you read just one book on Christ's ascension, make it this one. Highly recommended!"

—**J. Scott Duvall**, chair,
Department of New Testament,
Ouachita Baptist University

"I cannot remember the last time I heard a Christian talk about the ascension of Christ, let alone why it is indispensable to the Christian faith. But it is! Patrick Schreiner opens our eyes to a myriad of ways the ascension matters for Christ and his church. Apart from the ascension, Christ's authority as prophet, priest, and king is not vindicated, nor can he continue his intercession and reign from his heavenly throne, or build his church by his word and Spirit. Without the ascension we have no future hope either. So pick up and read this book. For not only is Jesus alive, but he reigns, guiding his church until one day we ascend with him in glory."

—**Matthew Barrett**,
associate professor of Christian theology,
Midwestern Baptist Theological Seminary,
and executive editor of *Credo Magazine*

THE ASCENSION OF CHRIST

THE ASCENSION OF CHRIST

RECOVERING A NEGLECTED DOCTRINE

Patrick Schreiner

SNAPSHOTS

MICHAEL F. BIRD, SERIES EDITOR

LEXHAM PRESS

The Ascension of Christ: Recovering a Neglected Doctrine
Snapshots, edited by Michael F. Bird

Copyright 2020 Patrick Schreiner

Lexham Press, 1313 Commercial St., Bellingham, WA 98225
LexhamPress.com

Print ISBN 9781683593973
Digital ISBN 9781683593980
Library of Congress Control Number 2020935536

Series Editor: Michael F. Bird
Lexham Editorial: Derek Brown, Claire Brubaker, Allisyn Ma, David Bomar
Cover Design: Brittany Schrock
Typesetting: ProjectLuz.com

To my children—Lydia, 9, Kesid, 7, Julianna, 5, and Canaan, 3.

Maybe this book is short enough that one day you will read it.

CONTENTS

PREFACE

My interest in the ascension was birthed in another project. As I composed an introduction to an Acts commentary, I argued for the centrality of the ascension in Luke's imagination. My sense was Paul and the rest of the New Testament writers sustained this stream of thought in their writings. I expanded my view a little and began to see the ascension everywhere. The continuing reign and life of the enthroned Christ is the theological core and narrative heart of Acts and the basis for the rest of the New Testament. It was not that I had denied the ascension before; I simply hadn't articulated its significance in my own thinking processes.

Because it had been helpful in my own study, when I met Derek Brown of Lexham Press at the famous Portland restaurant ¿Por Qué No? I pitched the idea of doing a book on the ascension, and Derek said, "Why not?" Thanks goes to Western Seminary, who allowed me time to work on this project, especially Chuck Conniry, who has been supportive of my writing projects. Thanks also to all who read the manuscript and made it much better than it was originally.

Derek Brown read it carefully and pointed out where my language or concepts were confusing. My father read an early draft, providing helpful exegetical suggestions. Peter Orr sent me an early version of his New Studies in Biblical Theology book and pointed out a few places I contradicted myself especially in regard to presence and absence. Tim Harmon clarified a few arguments from a systematic-theology perspective. My fellow pastor Jared Pulliam helped me distinguish between the ascension as a climax and Jesus' return as a climax. My colleague Ryan Lister provided helpful writing-style feedback and many comma insertions. Gerry Breshears pointed out places where I was less than clear. Matt Emerson did more than make sure I capitalized Pride Rock, but also did that. Bobby Jamieson sent me his work on Christ's heavenly work and challenged me to think more carefully about Christ's heavenly priesthood. Gavin Ortlund also pointed me to some resources he had either written or worked through. Phillip Howell noted some mistakes and pointed me to a few key articles.

My initial outline had Christ's activities identified as "empowering his witnesses, Christ's heavenly intercession, and installed as Lord." I changed it to "building his church, interceding in heaven, and reigning over all" because in our church we were using the Ligonier christological statement as our corporate confession. I found that these better summed up my points.

Finally, gratitude goes out to the baristas at Heart Coffee on Woodstock, where I spent most of my time writing. They endured me in their shop for long days and continual tea refills. The soundtrack for this book includes many Spotify playlists, but I kept returning to a few artists, who should also be thanked: The National, First Aid Kit, Amos Lee, Bon Iver, Vampire Weekend, LP, Ludovico Einaudi, Nicholas Britell, and Max Richter.

INTRODUCTION

The arc of the moral universe is long, but the Messiah's ascension determines its finale. However, the ascension is often overlooked. Yet, it is a key moment in the good-news story and a crucial hinge for Christ's threefold work as prophet, priest, and king. This book is a short attempt to give the Christ's ascent better narrative and theological positioning.

The ascension (rising) of Christ refers to Jesus going up from earth into heaven. His session (sitting) speaks of Christ sitting at the right hand of the Father. These are two closely linked stages of Christ's exaltation and triumph, but in a real sense the ascent is the *journey*, while sitting is the *goal*. I will largely view them as a singular script. They both install Jesus to glory and declare him to be triumphant. When I refer to the ascension, I imply the session. When I refer to the session, I imply the ascension.[1] Jesus ascends, sits, is currently sitting, and will come back to judge the quick and the dead.

My goal is to help people think through this piece of the Jesus event and impress its importance. I will do so not by tracing the whole story of the Scriptures, but by examining this event from

---

1. I will use a few terms interchangeably for stylistic purposes: "Christ"/ "Messiah," "ascension"/"session," "ascension"/"ascent." Though "ascension" speaks more to the doctrine and "ascent" to an event of upward movement, readers should not normally read into the word choice unless the paragraph or section calls for such a reading.

the perspective of the threefold office of the Messiah: prophet, priest, and king (*munus triplex*).

I structure it this way for three reasons. First, the threefold office highlights how Christ fulfilled key vocations in the old covenant. Second, all of these offices can also be viewed under the banner of "anointed offices," which fills out how Jesus is the Messiah. Finally, by examining these three offices, we can more precisely speak of Christ's exaltation and triumph.[2]

The basic assertion is the ascension is a key plot moment, a hinge on which Christ's work turns. It not only authorizes and endorses Jesus' work, but *continues* Christ's three roles. The ascent culminates Christ's earthly work and marks a shift in Christ's function as prophet, priest, and king. Gerrit Scott Dawson writes, "The ascension dynamically draws our attention to the *full range* of the present [and future] work of Christ."[3]

Before, Christ was prophet on the earth; now he builds his church as the prophet in heaven. Before, he was a priest on the earth; now he intercedes as our heavenly priest. Before, he was worshiped as the king of the Jews; now he has been installed as the Lord of heaven and earth.

Without the ascension, Christ's work is incomplete. Without the ascension, a huge hole stands open in the story. Without the ascension, other doctrines become skewed. My prayer is that this book will be a help to those who desire to know Christ's full work better and serve his people more faithfully.

---

2. The doctrine of Christ's threefold office was suggested by Eusebius and other Greek fathers, but John Calvin took it up and popularized it in Reformed thought. Some rightly add sage or teacher to the mix.

3. Gerrit Scott Dawson, *Jesus Ascended: The Meaning of Christ's Continuing Incarnation* (New York: T&T Clark, 2004), 9, emphasis added.

CHAPTER 1

OVERLOOKING THE ASCENSION

It is remarkable how little mention the ascension gets these days.
Once it was seen as the climax of the mystery of Christ. ...
Today it is something of an embarrassment.
—Douglas Farrow

PAUSING THE NARRATIVE

A few years ago, I started listening to audiobooks. One thing I immediately noticed with audiobooks is you end up stopping at odd junctures. I used the program when I was in the car, when I exercised, or when I got ready for the day. When that specific task was finished, it was time to hit pause.

This differs from reading a physical book, where typically a more natural ending point exists. With audiobooks, the hiatus might come at a key moment. I remember listening to the book *Ready Player One*. I pulled up to our house right when the protagonist said, "And then we all died."

The same thing can happen when we summarize the story of the Scriptures. We too can regularly hit the pause button on the scriptural story before key events occur. A focus on certain aspects can come at the expense of others.

Usually when I hear a gospel summary, I hear people mention Jesus' life, death, and resurrection. Rarely do I hear a whisper about the ascension. At times evangelicals have focused on the cross and the resurrection to the point that the ascent of Christ has been overshadowed. As Peter Orr states, "Christians have tended to focus their attention on what Jesus *has* done (his life, death and resurrection) and what he *will* do (return and reign)."[1] Studies on what Christ is doing now or what happened after the resurrection are relatively rare.

However, if the ascension resolves the narrative, if it confirms Christ's authority, if it is a vital step to bring the story full circle, if it is central to Christ's work and Trinitarian theology, then we need to embrace it and teach it often.

FIVE REASONS THE ASCENSION IS NEGLECTED

This first chapter recounts five reasons for the neglect of Christ's ascension and then five reasons we need to focus our attention on this central event.

THE BIBLE SPEAKS LITTLE OF IT

Christ's ascent can be overlooked for many reasons, but one of the most obvious reason is that it seems that the Bible speaks little of it. Nowhere does the New Testament use the customary Greek word for "ascent" (*anabasis*). Only two places in the

---

1. Peter Orr, *Exalted above the Heavens: The Risen and Ascended Christ*, New Studies in Biblical Theology 47 (Downers Grove, IL: IVP Academic, 2019), 1.

Scriptures narrate the event—the end of Luke and the beginning of Acts (Luke 24:50-53; Acts 1:9-11). The ascension narrative account covers a mere seven verses in the Bible, which, if you are counting, is 0.03 percent of all the verses in the Scriptures.

Some readers might be surprised to hear the end of Matthew does not portray Jesus ascending. The original conclusion to Mark does not include anything about it, and at the end of John, Jesus is still on the earth. Even Paul's list of what is of first importance does not include the Messiah's ascent (1 Cor 15:1-2). If this is a key part of the narrative, then why do the other Gospel writers not include it? Why is it given so little space in the narrative? Why is the word never used? And why does Paul not give it first importance?

IT SEEMS LIKE A BAD PLAN

The second reason the ascension can be neglected is that it can appear to be a bad plan. Jesus remaining on the earth seems intuitively like a better idea. This can be seen by the following premises and conclusions:

- Premise 1: Being with Jesus bodily in the new heavens and earth is the best end state.

- Premise 2: Jesus is no longer with us in his body.

- Conclusion: It would have been better if he had not left.

In some ways, the ascension appears like the worst plan ever. Jesus' life is good. Jesus' death is good. Jesus' resurrection is good. Jesus' ascension … we have questions. If Jesus were here on earth, a number of things would be easier. Take evangelism, for example. Talking to people about this figure who is long gone is not the easiest sell. But if Jesus were still on earth, it might be easier to convince people of his importance. We live in a world that prizes and prioritizes physical proof. People want tangible evidence for claims—not assertions impossible to prove.

People may also think it would be better if he were on earth because he could be more of a comfort to us. If Christ were physically beside us, his comforting hand would be with us as we go through sorrows. Currently, we must to pray to a Savior we cannot see and many times cannot hear. My children consistently ask me why God cannot come and show himself to us so that they can obtain more confidence. If we are honest with ourselves, we feel the same way. The Messiah's ascent can seem like a bad plan.

THE IMPLICATIONS ARE UNCLEAR

The third and related reason people disregard Christ's ascent is that it is hard to know why the event was necessary. The meaning of the ascension is a little blurry, or maybe it is our eyes. Why did he need to ascend? Was the resurrection not enough?

The disciples fell into this mode of thinking after Jesus' resurrection. Before Jesus ascended they asked, "Are you going to restore the kingdom to Israel at this time?" (Acts 1:6). They were not expecting the ascension. Was now the time when Jesus would set up his kingdom and conquer the forces against them? Maybe that is why they were caught staring into heaven and the angel told them to get to work. What they thought and hoped for was not as they imagined. Jesus was not supposed to leave, according to their plan.

Complicating it even more, the only two scriptural passages recounting the ascension contain little theological explanation for the purpose of the ascent (Luke 24:50–53; Acts 1:9–11). Modern readers find themselves staring into the heavens alongside the disciples with confused looks on their faces. This lack of explanation has sent interpreters on a search for the purpose and goal of Christ's ascent. As I will show as we proceed, the rest of the Scriptures do fill this out for us, but the reasons are not all located on the same page, nor in the same Testament.

THE EVENT IS ABNORMAL

The fourth reason the ascension can be deserted is that the event is objectively strange and outlandish from a modern perspective. In the days following Galileo and astrophysics, Newton and neural exploration, Copernicus and cloning, the ascent seems ridiculous. The ascension involves a middle-aged man going up into the air (maybe fast, maybe slow, but I like to think at medium speed) and disappearing into the clouds. Where did he actually go? With our modern scientific worldview, we know he must have traveled through the atmosphere, and then what? And how did he survive without a NASA space suit?

Even if you accept supernatural healings and the resurrection from the dead, those miracles make more sense because people can then live restored lives. The disciples were left gaping into the heavens not knowing what to do. He did not die this time—he left. Though we like to think we are different from the disciples, we can find ourselves also staring into the sky wondering what has happened and why this event was necessary.

THE RESURRECTION SUBSUMES THE ASCENSION

The final—and maybe most influential—reason the ascension gets neglected is that the Scriptures sometimes conceptually combine the resurrection and ascension. They at times slide seamlessly from Jesus' death to his glory, with the resurrection and ascension both included in the latter category. Luke 24:26 recounts how Jesus said the Christ would suffer and then enter into his glory. Luke moves quickly from Jesus' death to his glorious state. Paul in Philippians 2:8–9 pivots from the cross straight to the Christ's exaltation. Peter spent a significant amount of time in his first sermon on the fact that "God raised [Jesus] up" (Acts 2:24, 32). But all of Acts 2:24–36 is about the resurrection-ascension, sometimes making it hard to distinguish between the two.

In the apostles' minds, the upward movement of Jesus rising from the dead continued in the ascension. As John Webster states, "Resurrection, ascension and heavenly session together constitute the declaration or manifestation of the lordship of Jesus Christ."[2] This could help explain why some people speak of the resurrection and then stop.

However, a harmful underside lurks beneath this. When most readers see these texts, they think only of the resurrection. This is not wrong; it is simply incomplete. When the New Testament writers refer to the exaltation, they think of the completed act of resurrection-ascension as a whole. But when we say "exaltation," we are more prone to think only of the resurrection. Dawson rightly affirms in response, "The resurrection requires an ascension to be completed."[3] To put this another way, we cannot equate the resurrection with Christ's *full* glorification. If the resurrection fully confirms Jesus' lordship, then the ascension becomes an anticlimax. We can have the tendency to cut off what is implicit in the apostles' presentation and only speak of the resurrection.[4]

---

2. John Webster, *The Domain of the Word: Scripture and Theological Reason* (London: T&T Clark, 2014), 34.

3. Gerrit Scott Dawson, *Jesus Ascended: The Meaning of Christ's Continuing Incarnation* (New York: T&T Clark, 2004), 4.

4. Andrew Murray understands the ascension to be one of four pillars on which the church is built. "Faith has in its foundation four great cornerstones on which the building rests—the Divinity of Christ, the Incarnation, the Atonement on the Cross, the Ascension to the Throne. The last is the most wonderful, the

The biblical authors viewed Christ's act of rising as incomplete until Christ sat on his glorious throne. As Michael Horton says: we typically "treat the ascension as little more than a dazzling exclamation point for the resurrection rather than a new event in its own right."[5] Though the ascension might seem like another affirmation of God's victory, the ascension represents progress—a new stage—in Christ's exaltation, where he exercises his threefold office (prophet, priest, king) in a climactic way.

CONCLUSION

It might seem as if the Bible speaks little of the ascension. It might appear to be a bad plan. The implications might be unclear. The event may seem abnormal. And the resurrection can subsume the ascension. Yet, the ascension ultimately poses the question of the permanent centrality of Christ. If Christ is gone, is he still fundamental to work on the earth, or are we now simply in the age of the Spirit?

Christ's ascension and session needs better narrative and theological positioning. Without it, the story of Christ's work is incomplete. Without it, other doctrines become misaligned. Without it, our good news is truncated. Without it, Christ is not declared Lord and Messiah. The Son of God did not come down to earth to stay. He arrived in order that he might return, and then return again.

---

crown of all the rest, the perfect revelation of what God has made Christ for us. And so in the Christian life it is the most important, the glorious fruit of all that goes before." Andrew Murray, *The Holiest of All* (Springdale, PA: Whitaker House, 1996), 46.

5. Michael Horton, *People and Place: A Covenant Ecclesiology* (Louisville: Westminster John Knox, 2008), 3.

FIVE REASONS NOT TO
NEGLECT THE ASCENSION

The rest of the book will argue that we cannot, that we must not, abandon the ascension. For now, I turn to five crucial reasons not to neglect the ascension. These pave the way for the rest of the book, where I will explain the theological significance of the Messiah's ascent to the Father.

THE ASCENSION IN THE NEW TESTAMENT

Though Scripture narrates the ascension in only seven verses and the Greek word for "ascent" does not occur in the New Testament, these details can be misleading. Verbs that describe the ascension are plentiful. Consistently terms occur in reference to Jesus' ascent: "to go up," "to go away," "to go into," "to go through," "to sit," "to be taken up," or "to be exalted."[6] In addition, references to the repercussions of the ascension are ubiquitous in the New and Old Testaments.[7] Though the specific word "ascent" does not occur, the idea of exaltation and triumph is pervasive. All of what is written in the New Testament stems from the life, death, resurrection, *and* ascension of Jesus.

While Luke alone directly narrates the ascension, this does not mean the other Gospels lack the ascension. In Matthew's passion narrative, Jesus predicted the event: "You will see the Son of Man seated at the right hand of Power and coming on the clouds of heaven" (Matt 26:64). More notably, the end of Matthew contains two clear clues of Matthew's acknowledgment of the

---

6. "To go up": John 3:13; 6:62; 20:17; Acts 2:34; Eph 4:8–10; "to go away": Luke 24:51; John 7:33; 8:14, 21; 13:33; 14:4; 16:5, 7, 10, 17; "to go into": Heb 6:20; 9:12, 24; "to go through": Heb 4:14; "to go": John 14:2, 12, 28; 16:7, 28; 1 Pet 3:22; "to be taken up": Luke 24:51; Acts 1:2, 9, 11, 22; 1 Tim 3:16; "to sit": Eph 1:20; Heb 1:4; 8:1; 10:12; 12:2; "to be exalted": Heb 7:26.

7. I will focus on the NT here, because in the rest of the work I will display how the OT foreshadows the ascent of Christ in his three roles.

ascension (28:16–20). First, the command to go to all nations in Matthew 28:16–20 mirrors the command in Luke 24:47, which connects Jesus' instructions to his ascent. Second, readers attuned to the Old Testament will perceive that Matthew indirectly refers to the ascension in Jesus' last words: "All authority in heaven and on earth has been given to me" (Matt 28:18). This alludes to Daniel 7:13–14, which recounts the ascent of the Son of Man.

Mark's ending is no different, though he shocks and surprises. He intentionally leaves readers wondering what will come after the resurrection, which in its own way anticipates a further act (Mark 16:8). John's Gospel contains the most references to the ascension. The Fourth Gospel emphasizes the Son's unique relation to the Father and how he came from him and will return to him. Six times Jesus references going to the Father (John 14:9, 12, 28; 16:10, 17, 28), four times he makes reference to his ascent (1:51; 3:13; 6:62; 20:17), once to departing to the Father (13:1), and once to leaving the world and going to the Father (16:28). All of these naturally point to the ascension weighing heavily on John's mind.

The rest of the New Testament "thinks and speaks from this point, with a backward reference" to the ascension of Jesus Christ, as Karl Barth puts it.[8] The New Testament writings were birthed from the revelation and confirmation of Jesus' work. One of the surest markers of the ascension in the Epistles involves the titles most attributed to Jesus: Lord and Messiah. These became the designations all the New Testament authors use for describing Jesus. Because he had been enthroned, he was now recognized as the "Lord Jesus" or "Jesus the Lord" and

---

8. Karl Barth, *Church Dogmatics* (Edinburgh: T&T Clark, 1932–1967), IV.15.2, 134.

many times just "Lord" (Acts 2:36). His new name was Lord and Messiah because he had been properly exalted.[9]

Other references to Christ's ascent are peppered across the Epistles. Paul brings the resurrection and ascension together in 1 Corinthians 15. Twice in the passage following 15:1–2 he alludes to Christ's ascent by referring to Christ's present reign over every power and authority and reigning until he has put all his enemies under his feet (15:24–25).[10]

In 2 Corinthians Paul speaks of the judgment seat of Christ, implying Jesus currently sits on the throne (2 Cor 5:10). Ephesians largely concerns Christ's triumph and continually references how he is seated in the heavenly places (Eph 1:20; 2:6; 4:8–11). Philippians centers on Christ's ascent in the famous hymn, where it briefly recounts Christ's humiliation and exaltation (Phil 2:5–11). Colossians compels readers to seek the things above, "where Christ is, seated at the right hand of God" (Col 3:1). First Timothy 3:16 recounts Christ's life in a creedal formula ending with his reception into glory. Hebrews largely concerns Christ's current ministry as the exalted priest in the heavenly sanctuary (Heb 1:8; 4:14, 16; 6:19–20; 8:1; 9:12, 24; 12:2), and 1 Peter connects Christian baptism to Christ's ascent (1 Pet 3:21–22). Overall, the ascension looms large in the Epistles. It was not cast aside, nor ignored. Rather, it became the ballast for Christ's present work and his future judgment, and the basis for Christian ethics.

John's visions in Revelation, not surprisingly, also center on the one he sees in the throne room (Rev 1:13). In the Spirit John sees the throne and one seated on the throne, who receives glory,

---

9. Jesus is also called the "head" specifically in reference to his authority over the church and over the principalities and powers (Eph 1:20–23; Col 1:18; 2:10).

10. Phillip Howell pointed this out to me.

honor, and strength (4:2, 9–10). Between the throne and the four living creatures and among the elders, John sees a slain Lamb standing (5:6). The Lamb is with God and is worshiped in the throne room (5:13).[11]

Although the ascension is rarely mentioned in explicit terms, the New Testament assumes its central place. All of the authors write in response to, and work backward from, the ascension. The ascension revealed the Messiah's exaltation and triumph, finished his work on the earth, guaranteed his current sovereignty, broke the barrier between heaven and earth, thus pouring out the Spirit, and pledged his return. New Testament authors employ the event to comfort their readers, call them to holiness, and help them to endure suffering. Without the ascent of Christ, Christianity would not exist.

THE ASCENSION IN THE FIRST CHRISTIAN SERMONS

Not only does the New Testament as a whole provide evidence of the centrality of the ascension, but so do the first Christian sermons in Acts. When the apostles went out and preached the message of Jesus, they highlighted the resurrection and ascension. All five of Peter's sermons reference, either explicitly or implicitly, the ascension, and so do most of the speeches in Acts.

Peter's first sermon sets the stage for the rest of the sermons in Acts and provides one of the fullest summaries of the Christian message. In many ways, the rest of the sermons in Acts are condensed forms of the same themes. When Peter preached after Pentecost, he devoted a large portion of his sermon to the event of the resurrection/ascension of Christ. The same emphasis occurs in the rest of Peter's sermons. In Acts 3, after healing

---

11. Other references to Jesus' ascent and throne abound in Revelation (12:5; 14:4; 20:4, 11; 22:1; 22:3).

the lame man, Peter explained the healing did not come from his own power but from God. He affirmed heaven must receive Jesus until God restores all things (3:21). Later, in 4:10, Peter spoke of God raising Jesus from the dead and said salvation is found in no other name (4:12).

After Peter's second arrest, he again referenced the ascent, claiming, "God exalted this man to his right hand as Prince and Savior. ... We are witnesses of these things, and so is the Holy Spirit" (Acts 5:31–32). Peter's final sermon to Cornelius has at least two references to the Messiah's exaltation. He claimed Jesus is Lord of all (Acts 10:36) and said Christ "is the one appointed by God to be the judge of the living and the dead" (Acts 10:42).

Paul's sermons, like Peter's, also focus on the ascension. Paul's first sermon in Antioch sets the stage and informs the rest of the summaries Luke provides (Acts 13:16–41). Paul referred to Christ's ascension by quoting from Psalm 2. God raised Jesus up and Jesus became God's Son, as quoted in Psalm 2:7. The next verses continue Paul's theme about the exaltation of Jesus, but from a negative point of view: Jesus will not see decay (13:34–37). This is the same text Peter cited in his Pentecost sermon (2:25–28).

Paul and Silas told the prison guard in Philippi to believe in the Lord Jesus (16:31). Even in Antioch, when Paul preached to gentiles, he twice referenced Jesus' resurrection/ascension (17:18, 31). In Paul's farewell speech at Ephesus, he referred to faith in the Lord Jesus (20:21). The point is, when the early church proclaimed Jesus, it proclaimed his exaltation.

THE ASCENSION AS A CANONICAL HINGE

Third, the Messiah's ascent is a key to the scriptural narrative because of its canonical placement. Though the ascent is explicitly narrated in only two places, at the end of the Gospel of Luke (24:50–53) and at the beginning of Acts (1:9–11), these locations are quite important. If Acts pushes readers into a new phase of the story of God's work in this world, then at the center of this shift is the departure of Christ. The ascension marks the birth of a new age—the new covenant—and the end of the old era.

On the dime of the ascension, the Bible transitions from the age of Jesus to the age of the church. The development of all the other themes in the New Testament is sourced in the reality of Christ's enthronement and the Father's plan. As Robert Maddox puts it, "The ascension is for Luke the point of intersection of Christology, eschatology, and ecclesiology."[12]

Christ's ascension and session therefore became the hinge on which the New Testament turns—a watershed moment determining and directing the rest of the narrative. A few explorations of how this canonical hinge informs the reading of the rest of the New Testament are necessary.

First, *the gospel*, which brings salvation, directly concerns Jesus' reign over all. Jesus was declared the king of the universe because of, or maybe better, *in* his ascent. This Son of Man was given dominion, glory, a kingdom that all peoples, nations, and languages should serve him; his kingdom is one that will not be destroyed (Dan 7:13–14). The exaltation and dominion of Christ was not only the spur catapulting his people into the world but the message they were to share. Thomas Torrance writes, "The church lives and works in the time that is established by the ascension for the proclamation of the gospel to all nations and ages."[13]

---

12. Robert Maddox, *The Purpose of Luke-Acts* (Edinburgh: T&T Clark, 1982), 10.

13. Thomas F. Torrance, *Atonement: The Person and Work of Christ*, ed. Robert T. Walker (Downers Grove, IL: IVP Academic, 2014), 304.

Second, *the place* of Jesus' reign became the ground for mission to the ends of the earth. The rest of the New Testament essentially recounts the growth and struggle of these Jesus communities as they popped up all over the Greco-Roman world. They spread out *because* Jesus reigns in heaven. The spread of the gospel *geographically* and the birth of the church is inseparable from Christ's cosmic reign in the heavens. Earthly space was reordered by the heavenly Christ. Christ's reign in heaven became the primary setting for the New Testament, forming the theological and narratival perspective for the rest of the story. Without the ascension there would be no mission.

Third, the ascended Lord and the Father *sent the Holy Spirit* to his people. The rest of the New Testament explains and encourages Christians in the way they can be continually filled with the Spirit. This can only happen because of Christ's ascent. Peter in his Pentecost sermon explained how Jesus' ascension and pouring out of the Spirit were linked: "Being therefore exalted at the right hand of God ... he has poured out this that you yourselves are hearing and seeing" (Acts 2:33).

THE ASCENSION IN THE CREEDS

The fourth reason to not abandon the Messiah's ascension is the fathers of the faith made it central and foundational in the early creeds. Whenever the early Christians recounted the work of Christ in summary form, the ascension was always included.

The Apostles' Creed (AD 120-250) includes the ascent in the narrative summary of Jesus' work. The creed includes the line "he ascended into heaven, he is seated at the right hand of the Father." Jesus' work, according to the early creed, culminates in Christ's ascension and session in heaven, from which he will come again to judge the living and the dead. The Nicene Creed (AD 325) similarly speaks of Christ's work, which concludes and climaxes with the ascension. The Son was made incarnate, suffered, rose from the dead, and "ascended into heaven. From thence he shall come to judge the quick and the dead."

The First Council of Constantinople (AD 381) includes his incarnation, birth, crucifixion, burial, and resurrection. It does not abandon the Messiah's ascent, asserting he "ascended into heaven, and sits at the right hand of the Father, from where he will come again, with glory, to judge the quick and the dead; whose kingdom shall have no end." The Chalcedonian Creed (AD 451) focuses on the double nature of Christ and therefore does not recount the narrative of Christ's life in any way. The Athanasian Creed (AD 500), though focused on Trinitarian doctrine and Christology, includes a summary of Christ's life. Like the earlier creeds, it includes a clause about Christ's session. "He ascended into heaven, he sits at the right hand of God the Father Almighty, from where he will come to judge the living and the dead."

The major Protestant confessions also include the ascent in their doctrinal statements. The Augsburg Confession (1530) states that Jesus "ascended into heaven, and sits at the right hand of God." The First Helvetic Confession (1536) says, "He has set his flesh, which he raised from death to life, at the right hand of his almighty Father." The Scots Confession (1560) asserts Christ "did ascend into the heavens, for the accomplishment of all things, where in our name and for our comfort He has received all power in heaven and on earth, where He sits at the right hand of the Father."

In summary, when the church creeds recount the basic narrative of Christ's work, they *always* include the ascent. The ascension and session is the triumph of Christ's story. Early Christians never overlooked or disregarded the exaltation of Christ in confessional documents. Christ's ascension and session constantly came after Christ's resurrection and before the statement that he will return to judge the living and the dead.

THE ASCENSION IN THEOLOGY AND PRACTICE

The final reason the Messiah's ascent is essential is its relation to other doctrines and its practical significance. The last chapter will deal more fully with the relationship of the ascension to other doctrines, but for now it is important to recognize it is fundamentally a Trinitarian reality. In the ascension Jesus returned to the Father (John 16:28; 20:17), and they both bestowed the Spirit (Acts 2:33). Any reading of our Bible that neglects the christological center or the Trinitarian nature of this work will be fundamentally skewed from the start.

At a practical level, the ascension had wide application, both personal and corporate. The church conducts its new citizenship in response to the absence and in anticipation of the return of Christ as king and judge. The two angels in Acts 1:11 declared Jesus would come back in the same way he was taken up. Torrance says, "By withdrawing himself from continuing visible and immediate contact as our contemporary in history, Jesus Christ establishes the people of God within the process and structured patterns of history as a coherent body."[14] Christ's kingdom is here, progressing, and will come again. It is localized in the work of the church through the Spirit.

The ascension is cosmic (the reign of Jesus in the heavens), political (Jesus is Lord), and liturgical (the church enacts this movement in its rituals) in scope. Jesus' rule over heaven and earth is the foundation for our witness on the earth. His lordship is what we call others to bow before. And the actions of the church mimic a descent-ascent pattern. We go underwater

---

14. Torrance, *Atonement*, 295.

that we might be raised up. We suffer that we might be glorified. We sacrifice that we might be accepted. We bear one another's burdens so that we might experience the presence of God. We go down with Christ that we might rise with him. Christ is our brother, and we follow him into fullness of life.

CONCLUSION

The Messiah's ascent is thus critical for any reading of the Bible. It is a vital hinge on which the work of Christ turns. Though it can be overlooked and even neglected, Christ's ascension was central to the New Testament, the early creeds, the first Christian sermons and the transition from the Jesus age to the church age, and has theological and practical significance.

To avoid distorting our Bible reading, the rest of this book will look to Christ's threefold office under the shadow of the ascended Messiah. The ascension culminated Christ's earthly work and marks a shift and climax in the Messiah's three key roles. It not only *confirms* Christ's work but *continues* Christ's work. He once labored on the earth; now he labors in heaven. Jesus previously possessed these stations, but his session was the "definitive—irrefutable—declaration of his inherent dignity."[15]

The following chapters will follow a simple outline. I will

1. show how Jesus is portrayed as a prophet, priest, and king on the earth;

2. briefly examine the portrait of prophet, priest, and king in the Old Testament, providing categories for how Christ's work crowns these roles;

---

15. Webster, *Domain of the* Word, 34.

3. look to Old Testament stories that indicate an impending shift in these offices;

4. explain how the ascension marks a turn in the Messiah's work as he now accomplishes these vocations from heaven; and

5. consider how the church continues and extends the threefold office after the ascension.

CHAPTER 2

ASCENSION OF THE PROPHET

Building His Church

I will not leave you as orphans; I will come to you.
—John 14:18

EMPOWERING FOLLOWERS

One of my favorite movies of all time is *Hook*. I have seen it far too many times. *Hook* recounts the story of businessman Peter Banning, who has forgotten his past life in Neverland. However, Captain Hook wants his old formidable foe back and therefore captures Peter's children and brings them to Neverland.

Peter must travel back to Neverland and remember his old self. While he has been gone, a new leader has taken the reins: Rufio. When Peter arrives, he trains under the tutelage of the Lost Boys. They help him get into shape and stir his elapsed imagination.

The climax of Peter's training comes the day he relearns to fly. As Peter ascends into the sky, Rufio realizes the time has come for power to transfer.[1] Rufio climatically falls down on his knees before Peter's feet and offers him his old sword. He stands up and says, "You are the Pan. You can fly, you can fight, and you can crow." Then he joins the other Lost Boys as they dance and crow around Peter Pan.

This is an ascension scene. But what follows is an empowering and building project. As Rufio offers the sword, the Lost Boys are again united to their former days of glory under their realized leader. Peter's ascent to his former glory does not terminate his calling; it fulfills his role. Peter joins the Lost Boys as they gather around him, but does so now in a different way. He is no longer Peter Banning, but Peter Pan.

However, Peter will not go off and fight Captain Hook alone. In his ascent he empowers the Lost Boys to carry his work in Neverland with him as their leader. His presence both resides with them and transcends their experience. He, and he alone, can fly. The Lost Boys now enjoy the authority of their soaring leader among them, and they can go out in confidence because their leader has been granted all authority, dominion, and power.

While the analogy breaks down at certain points, this scene illustrates what happens at the ascent with Christ's prophetic office. As Jesus ascended, he received power. This did not halt his prophetic task; his prophetic commission was realized in a new way. Through rising, he empowered his people and unified them under his sovereign voice. He gave them his Spirit and authorized them to go forward in his prophetic work.

The ascension therefore culminates or crowns Christ's prophetic work, but also recommences it for a new era. Now his

---

1. Samuel James reminded me of this scene.

people are empowered to carry on his prophetic work because Christ's presence is mediated to them by the Spirit. The ascension needs better narrative positioning because Christ's prophetic work has not ceased—it has been thrust into a higher gear.

THE PROPHET JESUS

When Jesus walked on this earth, how did people see him? What images surfaced in their mind as he healed and proclaimed the kingdom of God? Christians are probably prone to think of Jesus as the Son of God, the second person of the Trinity who took on human flesh, true God and true man. He is the Christ, the Messiah. This is natural, for the Epistles rarely, if ever, explicitly label Jesus a prophet—he is consistently christened as the Messiah.

However, this is not what Jews initially thought about Jesus as he trudged the dusty paths of Nazareth in Galilee. They had a category to put him in, but not the "Son of God" or "Christ." While there certainly were diverse responses to Jesus, one of the primary concepts that arose in the minds of those in the first century was Jesus as *a prophet*.

The Gospel writers portray Jesus as a prophet from the beginning to the end of their works. Though many differences persist between the four Gospels, they collectively begin by portraying John the Baptist as the forerunner to Jesus. John the Baptist is distinctly decorated as a prophet; he performed the actions of a prophet (Matt 3:1; Mark 1:4; 6:14; John 1:15) and dressed as a prophet (Matt 3:4; Mark 1:6); the crowds and disciples identified him as a prophet (Matt 21:26; Mark 8:28; 11:32; Luke 9:19; 20:6); and Jesus correlated the Baptist with other prophets (Matt 16:14). For the Gospel writers, John the prophet prepared the way for Jesus the prophet. John was the last old-covenant prophet, while Jesus' prophetic work unlocked a new era.

Jesus also affirmed with his own mouth that he was a prophet. "A prophet is not without honor except in his hometown and in his own household" (Matt 13:57; see also Mark 6:4; Luke 4:24; John 4:44). Jesus quoted from Isaiah 61 in Luke 4, saying the Spirit had anointed him to be a *herald* of God's good news. The crowds continually labeled Jesus as a prophet. When Jesus healed a dead man, the crowd glorified God, saying, "A great prophet has arisen among us!" (Luke 7:16). When Jesus came into Jerusalem, the city asked, Who is this figure? The crowd affirmed, "This is the prophet Jesus, from Nazareth of Galilee" (Matt 21:11). When the religious leaders sought to arrest Jesus, they feared the crowds because they held him to be a prophet (Matt 21:46). Then, when Jesus asked his disciples what the people thought of Jesus, they said, "Some say John the Baptist, others say Elijah, and others Jeremiah or one of the prophets" (Matt 16:14; see also Mark 8:28).

In summary, Jesus came to the earth as more than a prophet—but not less. He arrived, as N. T. Wright puts it, "like the prophets of old, coming to Israel with a word from her covenant god, warning her of the imminent and fearful consequences of the direction she was travelling, urging and summoning her to a new and different way."[2] He fulfilled the role of the promised prophet (Deut 18:18), affirming he was a prophet, and this label was the most common one given to him by the crowds and religious leaders. If Jesus' ascension authorized and endorsed his threefold office, then we must ask how the ascent shifted Jesus' prophetic work.

PORTRAIT OF A PROPHET

To understand how Jesus fulfilled and even extended this prophetic role in his ascent, it is important to also get a sense of the prophetic task from the Old Testament and how Old Testament

---

2. N. T. Wright, *Jesus and the Victory of God* (Minneapolis: Fortress, 1996), 163.

prophets leaned forward to a day when a better prophet would arrive. Though many descriptions and explanations of prophets could be given, I limit myself to three: prophets were empowered by God's Spirit, proclaimed the word of God, and performed signs and wonders.

First, prophets had a radical encounter with God's presence and were empowered with the Spirit. Adam and Eve received the breath of God at creation (Gen 2:7). They both were to go out and be the mouthpieces for God in all of creation. Numbers 11:17 states that the Spirit rested on Moses. Moses even exclaimed his desire that Yahweh would put his Spirit on all of the people as he did for the seventy (11:29). The Lord told Isaiah the prophet his Spirit rested on him and therefore the Lord's words were in him:

> "My Spirit that is upon you, and my words that I have put in your mouth, shall not depart out of your mouth, or out of the mouth of your offspring, or out of the mouth of your children's offspring," says the LORD, "from this time forth and forevermore." (Isa 59:21)

When the Lord spoke to Ezekiel, the Spirit entered into him (Ezek 2:2; 3:24). Daniel had the Spirit of the holy God (Dan 4:8–9, 18; 5:11, 14). Finally, Micah said the Spirit of the Lord filled him (Mic 3:8). Prophets were those who were given the Spirit to perform the task of Yahweh on his behalf. As they were filled with the presence of God, they spoke the word of God and performed signs that pointed to God's attestation of their ministry.

Second, prophets proclaimed the word of God. They were truth tellers, delivering messages from God. When Moses was called, he hesitated because he was not eloquent of speech, but God told him he would speak through him (Exod 4:10–12). When the Lord called Samuel, the text says, "the LORD was with

him and let none of his words fall to the ground" (1 Sam 3:19).
Burning coals touched Isaiah's mouth, and he was told to *speak*
God's words to the people of Israel (Isa 6:6–9). The Lord spoke
to Jeremiah, saying he knew him and consecrated him before
he was born to be a prophet. But Jeremiah responded, "I do not
know how to speak, for I am only a youth" (Jer 1:5–6). God replied
that whatever he said Jeremiah would speak, and he touched
Jeremiah's mouth and gave him words (Jer 1:7–9). Ezekiel was
sent to a nation of rebels and told to speak the words of the Lord
(Ezek 2:3–4). The portrait of a prophet therefore must begin with
their speaking vocation. Prophets spoke messages of both hope
for Israel and doom if they neglected the covenant with Yahweh.
They pronounced blessings in the nations if they stayed loyal,
but woes if they began to worship the gods of other nations.

Third, prophets performed signs and wonders. Moses was
known for his signs and wonders (Exod 4:30; 11:10). In fact, when
Moses was called as the prophet to Israel, he was given signs to
convince Israel to listen to his voice (Exod 4:1–9). Jeremiah later
reflected that Yahweh brought Israel out of Egypt with signs and
wonders (Jer 32:21). Elijah performed many miracles: he caused
the rain to cease, raised a widow's son, provided food for the
starving, called fire down from heaven, and parted the Jordan.
Elisha resurrected the Shunammite's son, made an ax-head float,
and smited the Syrian army with blindness and gave them sight
again. Prophets therefore not only proclaimed the word of the
Lord, but confirmed this word by the signs and wonders.

While prophets were important figures, the Old Testament
also leaves this office wanting. Repeatedly prophetic imageries
point forward to a time when another prophet will come who
will fulfill the prophetic role in a more complete sense. While
God empowered his prophets to speak his word, the prophetic
role had a sense of incompleteness. False prophets arose, the

people did not listen to the prophet's voice, and the prophetic task was limited to certain individuals. Not all the people spoke the word of the Lord as the prophets. Moses cried out in Numbers 11:29, "Would that all the Lord's people were prophets." Israel longed for the day when another prophet would *rise up* (Deut 18:15).[3] A new day was coming where the Spirit's work would be realized.

Therefore, while all these attributes align with Jesus as *the prophet*, they also point to a day in the future when these marks of a prophet will enter a new era. While we tend to relegate the climax of Christ's prophetic work to his days on the earth, the biblical authors look at Christ's work as a whole. They intentionally expand Christ's prophetic work to both his earthly life and his continuing life in heaven. Already in the Old Testament there were shadow stories indicating a shift would occur. To these stories we turn.

SHADOW STORIES
OF THE PROPHET'S ASCENT

Jesus was known as the prophet who fulfilled the role of the Old Testament prophets while on earth. After the Messiah's ascent, this role did not cease. A shift transpired, but this alteration should have been expected. Key shadow stories in the Old Testament lead us to expect a shift in Christ's prophetic ministry.

The Old Testament prepares readers with succession, transferal, and ascension shadow stories. These shadow stories all predict a coming time when the prophetic work will enter a new era. A new prophet will arise, and he will complete the

---

3. While this language certainly points to Christ's incarnation, it should also be interpreted in terms of Jesus' ascension.

prophet portrait when he ascends to God. Three ascent stories reverberate with themes prefiguring a democratization of the prophetic task.

ADAM AND EVE ON THE MOUNTAIN

From page one of the Bible, God bequeathed his breath (spirit) to humanity so they could partner with him in his rule over creation and be his prophetic voice over creation. Though this might not appear to be a shift in the employment of the prophetic word, readers should remember at the beginning of creation only God spoke. After God created, a shift occurred. God bestowed this prophetic speaking task to his image bearers (men and women). They named the animals, and Adam declared Eve was fit for him.

Notably, Adam and Eve received God's word and spirit on a mountain—a high place. Genesis 2:8–14 says a single river flowed out of Eden but then became the source of other rivers as they flowed downhill. Ezekiel confirms this topography and calls Eden the garden of God and the holy mountain of God (Ezek 28:13–14). Joel 2:1–3 speaks of Mount Zion as like the garden of Eden. Eden was therefore the divine heaven-and-earth mountain-temple. At the top of the mountain Adam and Eve received God's word and breath. With this word they were to go and bestow the blessings of his voice over the whole creation. They were to go down from Eden and extend that word.

Therefore, already in the first few pages of the Bible, God made it clear his prophetic voice was be extended, given, and bestowed on his people. At the start of the biblical story, God gave his words to his people *on a high place* so that they might democratize God's word as they carried God's ruling voice in both their speech and deeds. With the arrival of sin, humans corrupted and twisted their prophetic task, but God graciously continued to use human beings as his mouthpiece. A future human would come who would ascend and be the fulfillment of the prophetic hope.

MOSES AND MOUNT SINAI

The democratization of God's word also appears when Moses ascended the mountain to receive the law. Though his ascent was exclusive, the purpose was to bring God's prophetic voice down to earth, found in the Torah. Moses rose up to bring God's word down. Upon coming down the mountain, he both delivered God's law to the people and brought with him God's presence. Though the law stipulated the presence of God must be regulated, Moses still delivered God's prophetic word and mediated God's presence.

As we have already seen in the prophetic portrait, prophets had the Spirit and delivered God's word. Before Moses' time, God's word came to God's people at various times and in various places. However, the Torah marked a new era when God's will was written down for all the people to follow. As Moses ascended into God's presence and delivered God's word, so too Jesus ascended into God's presence and confirmed God's word.

Moses did not cease existing as a prophet after he ascended the mountain. Rather, he ascended to deliver God's word to the nation so that they might be those who bless all nations. The nation as a whole was to embody this law of God and thereby act as prophets to the surrounding world. Moses, in this way, transferred and mediated the word of God to God's people, who now retained the responsibility to be loyal to this covenant.

While we can recognize a pattern in the stories of both Adam and Eve and Mount Sinai when Moses ascended the mountain, in each of these corruption seeped in. Adam and Eve listened to another voice, and their prophetic task was corrupted. At and after Sinai, the people continued to sin by not spreading God's prophetic voice and did not bless the other nations as they should have. God's aim was to democratize his prophetic voice. The Old Testament looks forward to a time when this pattern will be fulfilled and completed, and it will be joined with an ascent story.

ELIJAH ASCENDED AND GAVE ELISHA THE SPIRIT

A final key ascent story combined with the transfer of prophetic power occurs in 2 Kings 2. Elijah, the great prophet to the hardened Israel, was climatically taken up in a whirlwind to heaven, and Elisha, his prophetic protégé, received a double portion of his spirit. The narrative leading up to this scene is telling.

When Elisha asked for a double portion of his spirit, Elijah responded by saying this was a hard thing. Yet Elijah also affirmed it is possible, but mysteriously links it to Elisha *witnessing* Elijah's ascent. The double portion of his spirit would only be possible if Elisha witnessed Elijah being taken from him. If he saw, then he would receive Elijah's spirit, but if not, it would not be so (2 Kgs 2:10).

Two chariots of fire suddenly separated Elijah and Elisha, and Elijah went up by a whirlwind of heaven as Elisha watched. Fire, wind, and ascent again occur in a scene where prophetic power transfers. When Elijah was taken up on the chariots, his cloak dropped, and Elisha took the cloak and struck the water, and it parted in two. When the sons of the prophets saw this, they said, "The spirit of Elijah rests on Elisha" (2:15). It is an ascent, witnessing, and succession story. Only because Elisha had witnessed Elijah ascend, and only because he had taken up his coat, did the prophetic Spirit come on Elisha.

Readers should lay this story on Acts 1:9–11 and note the emphasis on the disciples witnessing Christ's ascent.

> After he had said this, he was taken up as they were *watching*, and a cloud took him out of their sight. While he was going, they *were gazing* into heaven, and suddenly two men in white clothes stood by them. They said, "Men of Galilee, why do you stand *looking up* into heaven? This same Jesus, who has been taken from you into heaven, will come in the same way that *you have seen him* going into heaven." (csb)

They watched, they gazed into heaven, and then the two angels came and said Jesus would come back in the same way. If the way to the garden was blocked by the flashing swords of the cherubim, then these two angels announced the way was broken open by Jesus. The prophetic Spirit of Jesus was poured out when they went to the Upper Room, where they received power from on high. At that point they were Jesus' prophetic witnesses in Jerusalem, in all Judea and Samaria, and to the ends of the earth (Acts 1:8). Their time to be filled with the Spirit and sent out into the nations had now arrived.

CONCLUSION

Though more episodes could be recounted, these three Old Testament stories demonstrate that God's prophetic work was always meant to include human beings. Adam and Eve were to be God's prophetic voice on the earth; Israel was to be a light to the nations; Elijah and Elisha were tasked with calling the nation back to the covenant. In each story, the democratization of the task and the gift of the Spirit is linked to an ascent. However, in each story it is also clear something was terribly wrong—the people needed the Spirit in a more complete way.

Christ arrived as *the prophet* who delivered God's word, performed signs and wonders, and possessed the Spirit on the earth. He fulfilled the old covenant by being *the* anointed Prophet. However, he also promised a time when he would leave and this prophetic task would continue and also be transferred to his people. It is not that he would not be involved; he would simply be involved in a different way after his ascent into heaven. Now it is time to look to Christ's ascent and the implications for Christ as our eternal prophet.

THE ASCENSION AND
CHRIST BUILDING HIS CHURCH

The Old Testament looked forward to a coming prophet, and Jesus fulfilled this role. Key Old Testament stories foreshadow a shift in the prophetic task. They indicate Jesus was not merely a prophet on the earth, but he continued in his prophetic role when he ascended into heaven. Now that Jesus is no longer here, he does not perform signs and wonders, nor speak the words of God in the same way. Neither is the Spirit-filled Jesus with us bodily. But this does not mean Christ's prophetic work was put on hiatus when he proceeded into heaven.

The ascent not only *authorizes*, but *amplifies* and *multiplies* his prophetic work. Because of the ascension, Christ sent the Spirit, continues to inspire his word, and fills and equips his church to perform his signs as his body on the earth. In all of these ways, Jesus birthed, builds, and grows his church as the ascended prophet. The Messiah's ascension is not something that can be subtly pushed to the side as if it does not matter; it was the exaltation and continuation of Christ's prophetic work.

SENDING THE SPIRIT TO ALL

As already indicated, the Old Testament leaned forward toward the day when all God's people would receive the Spirit in a climactic way, and this was often connected to some story of ascent. Not surprisingly, therefore, Jesus linked the gift of the Spirit with his exaltation. His ascension fulfilled the hopes of the gift of the Spirit and therefore the democratization of the prophetic task. Through the Spirit, the ascended prophet would build his church.

The Gospel of John emphasizes this theme and even argues it is better that Jesus goes away. In John 16:7, Jesus said, "It is for your benefit that I go away, because if I don't go away the Counselor will not come to you. If I go, I will send him to you" (CSB). Jesus affirmed that the coming of the Spirit depended on his going away. His bodily absence was better for the disciples, because when he left the Spirit would come upon them. Why is it better to possess the Spirit than for Jesus to remain on the earth? Two reasons present themselves.[4]

First, Jesus' leaving was superior because the incarnate Jesus was limited by space and time by virtue of his humanity. When he ascended, he went to heaven, the place of God, which transcends space and time, and sent his Spirit. Jesus could not be with all his followers in the same way on the earth. When he left the earth, his prophetic voice became cosmic in scope. With the arrival of the Spirit, Jesus' presence and words could fill the world in a more expansive way. To put this negatively, if Jesus were still on the earth, his words and presence would not be able to spread as they did after Pentecost.

---

4. Readers should balance these statements with the reality that Paul says it is better to depart and be with Christ (Phil 1:23) and he would rather be away from the body and at home with the Lord (2 Cor 5:8).

While we can question where Jesus went when he floated into the sky in front of his disciples, there is no need for us to think of him needing a space suit. His return to God was a return to the dwelling place of God, which should go beyond human notions of place. Heaven is not a locality in the way we think of dwellings. Rather, the Scriptures portray heaven as much as a *state* as a locality.[5]

John Calvin and Karl Barth note how biblical writers never thought of the presence of God or the ascension merely in our terms of space and time. When Christ ascended, he sat at the right hand of God, but that place is also *everywhere*—for God is everywhere. The reality of the ascension goes beyond our human comprehension. As Torrance affirms: "The ascension must be thought of as an ascension beyond all our notions of space and time, and therefore as something that cannot ultimately be expressed in categories of space and time."[6]

The ascension thus marks the return of Jesus from our place to God's place. In this sense, the ascension was the goal of the incarnation. In the incarnation, Jesus entered in the space-time continuum, while in the ascension Jesus transcended space and time "without ceasing to be man or without any diminishment of his physical, historical existence."[7] When Jesus ascended, he transported to the place of God. That which is finite and temporal (Christ's assumed human nature) was hypostatically united

5. Milligan asserts, "When we speak of our Lord's ascension into heaven we have to think less of a transition from one locality than of a transition from one condition to another." William Milligan, *The Ascension and Heavenly Priesthood of Our Lord* (Eugene, OR: Wipf & Stock, 2006), 26. A change of locality is implied, but this is not the only dimension to consider. Admittedly, traditional Reformed thinkers have argued heaven is a created location, while Lutherans believe Christ became omnipresent at the ascension.

6. Thomas F. Torrance, *Atonement: The Person and Work of Christ*, ed. Robert T. Walker (Downers Grove, IL: IVP Academic, 2014), 286.

7. Torrance, *Atonement*, 287.

to that which is infinite and eternal.[8] We must approach Christ's new state from both temporal and eternal perspectives.

Second, obtaining the Spirit was better because Jesus' ascent did *not* mean his absence in an exclusive sense; it actually means Jesus is now *more* present. Jesus affirmed it was more excellent for his followers to receive the Spirit because Jesus' presence on the earth and absence from the earth cannot be pitted against each other. Rather, these two concepts unexpectedly fit together.

Two texts from John help explain this apparent contradiction. In the Upper Room, immediately after referencing the Spirit's coming, Jesus said: "I will not leave you as orphans; I will come to you" (John 14:18). Then in John 14:28: "You heard me say to you, 'I am going away, and I will come to you.'" Both of these texts are odd at face value because they pair Christ's leaving with his coming. Jesus claimed *he* would leave and *he* would come to them.[9] The presence of the Spirit is the presence of Jesus.

By ascending, Christ was not absent in the fullest sense.[10] Rather, his presence is merely known in a different way. The ascent, in a real sense, did not represent the Messiah's removal *from* the earth, but his constant presence *on* the earth. Farrow writes, "The ascended Lord is not everywhere ... but he is everywhere accessible."[11] Swain puts it this way:

---

8. This line comes from Tim Harmon through John Webster.

9. Some people admittedly interpret these phrases in John as referring to Jesus' presence and appearance to his disciples after his resurrection.

10. Jesus is absent bodily since Christ remains localizable, as Orr states. Peter Orr, *Exalted above the Heavens: The Risen and Ascended Christ*, New Studies in Biblical Theology 47 (Downers Grove, IL: IVP Academic, 2019), 78.

11. Douglas Farrow, *Ascension and Ecclesia: On the Significance of the Doctrine of the Ascension for Ecclesiology and Christian Cosmology* (Grand Rapids: Eerdmans, 1999), 178.

Even if Jesus appears to be absent from his church, in one sense, he is, in fact, more profoundly and intimately present to the church, in another sense. For he is now in "heaven" with God—in the heaven which, according to the biblical tradition, is a symbol not only of God's transcendence and inaccessibility, but also of God's omnipresence. Paradoxically, being in heaven with God, Jesus is also present in the world in the way that God is present.[12]

The New Testament sometimes speaks of the Spirit as the *Spirit of Jesus*. It would therefore be imprecise to say Christ is no longer present after his ascent, but accurate to affirm Christ no longer resides bodily on the earth. The words of Jesus in John help interpreters to see the mediation of Christ's presence is not equal: the Spirit's mediation of Christ is not only good but superior.

The ascension is therefore good news because Christ now fills his people with his presence by the Spirit, and the Spirit transcends the boundaries of space and time. The prophetic works of Jesus are now carried out by his witnesses, who are empowered by his Spirit. What this means is not that Christ's prophetic work has ceased but the Spirit *of* Christ continues

---

12. L. Swain, *A New Dictionary of Theology*, 63 (cited by Farrow, *Ascension and Ecclesia*, 12). John Calvin puts it this way: "For Christ left us in such a way that his presence might be more useful to us. ... He withdrew his bodily presence from our sight, not to cease to be present with believers ... but to rule heaven and earth with a more immediate power. As his body was raised up above all the heavens, so his power and energy were diffused and spread beyond all the bounds of heaven and earth" (Calvin, *Institutes*, ed. John T. McNeill, trans. Ford Lewis Battles (Louisville: Westminster John Knox, 2006), 2.16.14 [522–23]). Torrance similarly says: "The ascension of Christ is thus an ascension to fill all things with himself, so that in a real sense he comes again in his ascension. He had to go away in one mode of presence that he might come again in his mode of presence" (*Atonement*, 291).

to radiate Christ.[13] The ascent of Christ unlocked a new era of Christ's prophetic work as he builds his church.

AUTHORIZING HIS WORD

The ascension and the coming of the Spirit underpins the continuing prophetic work of Christ in terms of the ministry of the word. With the exaltation of Jesus, Peter Toon writes, "revelation continues to occur in fullness ... more than this, it is strengthened."[14] The prophetic work of Christ should be connected not only to the Spirit, but to the gospel message—the word—which is found in the Scriptures. The ascended prophet builds and strengthens his church through his word.

If prophets were the ones who spoke the word of God, then we must ask how the word of God functions in this new era. To paraphrase John Webster, Christ resides over the Scripture and reveals himself in it, and therefore the word should be defined as the *creaturely auxiliary* of the exalted prophet's self-proclamation.[15] The word is a prophetic tool of Christ on the earth. In essence, Christ's prophetic work continues not only by the Spirit but in his word. The word becomes Christ's scepter through which his prophetic office continues.

Though people in the Old Testament heard words from God, Peter said now after Christ's ascension the word was more fully confirmed (2 Pet 1:19). Though prophets were also carried along by the Spirit in the Old Testament, the Old Testament prophets

---

13. Ferguson puts it this way: "Christ in his ascension came into such complete possession of the Spirit who had sustained him throughout his ministry that economically the resurrected Christ and the Spirit are one to us. He is *alter Christus*, another Christ, to us." Sinclair Ferguson, *The Holy Spirit* (Downers Grove, IL: InterVarsity Press, 1996), 54.

14. Peter Toon, *The Ascension of Our Lord* (Nashville: Thomas Nelson, 1984), 92.

15. John Webster, *The Domain of the Word: Scripture and Theological Reason* (London: T&T Clark, 2014), 38.

longed for the revelation of Christ (1 Pet 1:10–12). Jesus is God's Word (John 1:1). He is God's speech to us. He explains the Father (John 1:18; 14:9). God spoke to the fathers in the prophets, but in the last days he has spoken in his Son (Heb 1:1–2). In the new covenant, the apostles did not look forward to Jesus, but proclaimed the Jesus who had already come and is now Lord and Christ because he has risen to the right hand of the Father. The word, after the Messiah's ascent, was therefore authorized in a greater sense than before, because God's word was confirmed in Christ and his exaltation.

Christ also inspires his word because he is present through the dispersion of his word. The presence of Christ the prophet with his people continues to be a *communicative* presence.[16] Christ, as *the Word*, remains and now advances in a more expansive sense as the oral and written word disseminates through the ages. Jesus is therefore still active and present as the prophet, but not physically in the same sense. He is present *by* his Spirit and *in* and *through* his word. His word self-declares: it addresses both his people and the world, making himself known as the exalted prophet.

Though it can be tempting to still desire Jesus' physical voice addressed to us, John 16:7 ushers people away from this thought. The Messiah's ascent made his word more illuminating and more sure rather than less. The ascension, in this sense, was the final word, and without the final word, the story would be incomplete.[17] After the final act concludes, hearers can uniquely comprehend the nature of this story. Christ's ascent does not make

---

16. Webster, *Domain of the Word*, 35.

17. By saying "final word," I am not denying the consummation of history. The ascension begins the end.

his prophetic task cease, but makes it present in expansive times and places through both the Spirit and word.

EQUIPPING AND FILLING HIS CHURCH

Prophets were filled with the Spirit and proclaimed the word, but they also performed signs and wonders. But how does this aspect of the Messiah's prophetic task continue after his ascension? Through the church. Not only is the word Christ's prophetic *creaturely auxiliary*, but the church functions in a similar way.[18] Christians are Christ's tool (body) on the earth—the ones who perform his signs and wonders by his Spirit. Jesus' prophetic ministry thus continues after the ascension, yet in a different way. The followers of Jesus become the hands and feet of Jesus as they go out and speak about the Lord Jesus and perform signs and wonders, thus building and growing his church.

The Gospel of John contends the church will extend and expand the works of Jesus. Jesus affirmed, "Whoever believes in me will also do the works that I do; and greater works than these will he do, *because* I am going to the Father" (John 14:12). This statement has troubled interpreters over the centuries. However, the first thing to notice is this only kicks into reality at the Messiah's ascension.

"Greater" works likely refers to two realities. First, the church can more expansively spread Christ's work because it is more widely dispersed. Second, "greater" works refers to people's prophetic role after Jesus' completed work. They work in the time of fulfillment. "Greater" then refers to both extent and salvation-historical placement, which cannot be separated. Both of these points are secured by the Messiah's ascent to the

---

18. Not exactly the same, of course. God's word is inspired and always true. His people are still stained with sin.

right hand of the Father. As Christ's people are transformed by the word and Spirit, they become the prophetic hands and feet of Jesus.

Paul builds on this imagery in Ephesians, describing the head (Christ) as in heaven and his body (the church) as on the earth. Jesus, at his ascent, became the head over all things in the church (Eph 1:22). He is head of his prophetic body. He fills the church with his presence, and the church fills all things on the earth through its actions as its people are filled with Christ. The Messiah accomplishes this task through the gifts he gives the church. When Christ ascended, he gave the church apostles, prophets, evangelists, and teachers to equip the saints for the building of the church (Eph 4:10–12).

Christ's ascension, and his gifts, become the key for the church to be able fill all things. The church therefore becomes the *space* where Christ works as prophet. If he did not ascend to the place of Lord, the people would not have been filled with the Spirit to fill the earth with their words and deeds. The church should not be conceived of first as the body of Christ starting from earth and reaching heavenward. Rather, the body of Christ begins in heaven and reaches earthward. As his word and Spirit fill them, Christians carry Christ on their lips and in their hands.[19]

CONCLUSION

The Messiah's prophetic work did not cease at the ascension. Rather, it continued and even increased and multiplied in a more expansive but different way after Jesus was exalted. We have looked at three aspects of this prophetic mediation, which all relate to Christ building his church so that it might bless the

---

19. Milligan, *Ascension and Heavenly Priesthood*, 229.

world. He filled his people with his Spirit, he gave them his word, and he empowers them to be his hands and feet.

Prophetic Portrait	Before Christ's Ascent	After Christ's Ascent	Prophetic Concept
The Empowering Spirit	Jesus was filled with the Spirit	Christ poured out the Spirit from his exalted state, empowering his witnesses	The *mediation* of Christ's prophetic work
Proclaiming the Word	Jesus was and speaks the word of God	Christ continues to speak through the gospel and his Scriptures a word more fully confirmed	The *scepter* of Christ's prophetic work
Performing Signs and Wonders	Jesus performed signs and wonders	Christ became the head of his body, who are now his hands and feet on the earth	The *space* of Christ's prophetic work

1. At the Messiah's ascension, the Spirit descended to fill God's people, and they more expansively spread the presence of the prophet. Christ is not less present after his ascent; he is simply present in a different sense. As John Chrysostom states: "Heaven has the holy body and earth received the Holy Spirit."[20]

---

20. John Chrysostom, *Homilies on the Ascension* 2.

2. Jesus continues his prophetic work through the word found in the gospel message. Christ resides over the Scripture and reveals himself in it, and it all points to him. Christ as the prophet wields, inspires, and confirms his word as his scepter through which he declares himself and gives his charter to his church.

3. Jesus continues his prophetic work of signs and wonders through his creaturely auxiliary, called the church. The church is the space where Christ works as prophet. It is his body, which spreads out on the earth as people are filled with the Spirit and his word.

THE CHURCH AS PROPHETS

I began the chapter by recounting the scene in *Hook* when Peter Pan flies again and empowers and unites the Lost Boys. In a similar way, Christ's ascent has implications for the church's prophetic task. Farrow asserts neither the resurrection nor the Emmaus road event launched the church. "Its footings were laid on higher and firmer ground. ... Only with his establishment at the right hand of God ... did ecclesial being become possible."[21] If the prophetic office was fulfilled in the ascended Christ, then it is also fulfilled in his church. For the church is the body of Christ who by the Spirit enacts the will of its head on earth.[22] The people of the seated prophet are filled with the Spirit, proclaim the word of Christ, and perform signs and wonders.

---

21. Farrow, *Ascension and Ecclesia*, 10.

22. What I am not asserting is that the church and Christ are conflated; they are related while remaining distinct ideas. Christ's words are uniquely authoritative, and the church's teaching is based on Christ and can be flawed.

First, Christ's people are filled with the Spirit. Prophets had encounters with God and were filled with the Spirit. Pentecost is a prophetic text. For the biblical authors, Jesus' departure triggered Pentecost. Ascent and descent accompany each other. Jesus was *filled* with the Spirit; not until Jesus left could the Spirit come and empower Jesus' witnesses in the new covenant sense. The Spirit became the link between Jesus and his prophetic body. As Jesus rose into heaven, he pierced the barrier between God's realm and the human realm. He brought humanity into the presence of God and sent the divine down to the human level. In Acts 2, the Spirit descended at Pentecost and filled his disciples to be Jesus' prophetic voice.

Ephesians explicitly identifies the gifts the church received at the ascent to execute this task (Eph 4:7–12). Paul quotes from Psalm 68:18 to support the link between gifts and the spatial movement of Christ. Psalm 68:18 describes God's triumphal procession to his throne after leading his people out of Egypt. In a similar way, Christ triumphed over the cosmic forces of darkness, and as he did, he distributed the gifts of leaders in his church. As Christ was exalted, he therefore gave help to his people, by the Spirit, to battle the forces of darkness on the earth. The leaders of the church equip the saints in both their speech and actions.

Second, Christ contests the forces of darkness by giving verbal weapons of warfare to the church. Malevolent spiritual authorities battle against Christ's prophetic office by spreading their own good news. They distort and corrupt what God has said, as the serpent did in the garden. They promise a kingdom— but without Jesus as king. They convince humans that seizing the throne will mean fulfillment and life everlasting.

The officers of the church equip the army of Christ to prophetically proclaim that Jesus is Lord, opposing other messages of good news. The church dresses itself with the belt of truth, gospel shoes, the gospel of peace, and the sword of the Spirit (Eph 6:10–20). In helping the saints of local churches don this armor, church leaders equip them to go forth in the midst of battle looking to Christ the conqueror and declaring he is Lord and king.

The saints therefore continue Christ's prophetic work by acting as ambassadors of the good news of Jesus' death, resurrection, and ascension. They have the belt of truth and share the good news of Jesus' reign. Christians only declare Jesus is Lord by the power of the Spirit. When the Spirit came, he would bear witness about Christ (John 15:26–27), for the Spirit glorifies the Son (16:14). In the Scriptures, this proclamation of the good news is described as prophecy.

When the Spirit descended at Pentecost, the tongues of fire separated and rested on individuals, and they went out and prophesied in the name of Christ. Paul later said that believers should greatly desire to prophesy (1 Cor 14:1, 39). As John Calvin said, Jesus was anointed by the Spirit to be a prophet "not only for himself ... but for the whole body that the power of the Spirit might be present in the continuing preaching of the Gospel."[23] The church carries the prophetic cloak of Christ not by right but by gift.

Finally, the church functions as the prophetic arm of Jesus through actions—doing signs and wonders. The prophet Joel promised that at the turn of the ages (at Christ's session) wonders would be shown in the heavens above and signs on the earth below (Joel 2:30; Acts 2:19). As the apostles went out to spread Christ's prophetic word, they too performed signs and wonders (Acts 2:43; 6:8; 14:3; 15:12; Rom 15:19; 2 Cor 12:12). Throughout the

---

23. Calvin, *Institutes* 2.15.2.

New Testament the church is called not only to proclaim Christ, but to imitate Christ in his actions.

The people of God not only declare the truth of Jesus; they also receive the breastplate of justice, the shield of loyalty, and the helmet of salvation. In other words, the church does not merely put on the prophetic armor of God by speaking but by *acting* in the power of the Spirit for the good of God's people and the world.

In sum, the ascended Lord gave his people gifts so that they might continue his prophetic work on the earth. They are able to do so not because they possess great strength in themselves. Rather, they are able to do so as they look to their conquering prophet. They go forth into the world of darkness with the light of truth on their lips and the gospel of peace on their feet. Though false prophets will arise, Christ at his ascent gave the church leaders to proclaim and guard the doctrine of the gospel.

CONCLUSION

So what happened to Christ's prophetic work at the ascension? It did not cease. It was not put on hiatus. It was not marginalized, nor bottled up. Yet, it also does not continue in the same way. The ascension marks the end of our hearing his human voice speak on earth. He is gone.[24] But in another way it continues Christ's prophetic work in a new and better sense.

When Christ ascended into heaven, he transcended time and space, and therefore his absence resulted in the fullness of his presence through the Spirit. The Spirit has always been in the business of filling God's prophets with the word of Christ. At Pentecost this was no different, but now the Spirit was democratized and poured out on all people who submitted to Christ's

---

24. Farrow, *Ascension and Ecclesia*, 8.

lordship. The people of God were then filled with the Spirit, and they prophesied and performed wonders.

While the Spirit mediates Christ's prophetic work, the scepter Christ employs to continue his prophetic task is his word. He does so in the space of the church, which is Christ's body on the earth. His people are the creaturely auxiliaries through whom he now speaks and acts. As the church maintains its loyalty to Jesus, it becomes the realm of Christ's prophetic work.

As Farrow states,

> Through means of Word and sacrament, prayer and worship, the Holy Spirit presents the historical, ascended, and still advent Jesus to us freshly in the present moment. So, far from separating us from Jesus, the ascension makes the historical living Jesus ... our perennial meeting place with God until he returns.[25]

The Messiah's ascension was *and is* therefore good news. That is why Jesus could say it was better if he left earth (John 16:7) and that his disciples would do greater works than he did (14:12). For if he stayed with his disciples—if he stays with us—he could not be with us in the same way. But now that he has been enthroned above the earth, his prophetic work shifted, increased, multiplied, and expanded. Our mission is to continue Christ's work by the power of the Spirit, as we speak of Christ's exaltation and wait for his return.

Look to your ascended prophet.

---

25. Farrow, *Ascension and Ecclesia*, 51.

CHAPTER 3

ASCENSION OF THE PRIEST

Interceding in Heaven

> *He always lives to make intercession.*
> —*Hebrews 7:25*

INTERCESSION

In the middle of the first *Lord of the Rings* movie, Frodo is near to death from a Morgul-blade wound. He lies gasping in pain and dread—at the doorstep of death. Frodo has been stabbed in the shoulder, but Arwen has outrun the nefarious Ringwraiths who are in pursuit of Frodo. Now she seeks to get him to Rivendell to be healed.

She has brought him all the way to the far side of an elvish river, and as she watches him wheezing for life, she prays that any grace that she possesses might pass to him. Though the scene is not in the book (sorry, purists), it is an intimate moment of intercession. She willingly gives up what is hers for the sake of another.

Arwen is an interesting character in the Tolkien trilogy. She is a half-elf who forfeits her elvish immortality and remains in Middle-earth instead of traveling to the Undying Lands. The scene in the movie therefore rightly depicts her sacrificial, gracious, and intercessory ways. She sacrifices what is hers for the benefit of others. She does not grasp or exploit what is lawfully hers, but intercedes on behalf of others (Phil 2:5–11).

In a similar way, Jesus did not take advantage of his position but humbled himself by sacrifice. He rejected the path of glory and went through suffering and death so that he might intercede as the representative high priest. Jesus did travel to the Undying Lands. Yet, he traveled not only for his own sake. He sits at the right hand of God to intercede for his people.

Though he interceded for his people on the earth, now he intercedes by presenting his own blood before the Father. While Jesus was a priest on the earth, his priestly mission was exalted *and* endures after he ascends. At the ascension Jesus' *heavenly* intercession began—and his heavenly intercession is superior to his earthly office.

Because Christ currently presents his blood in the heavenly temple, we are able to also ascend the mountain of the Lord and enter into the throne room of God. The ascension is Christ's high-priestly act of intercession and blessing. The sacrifice has been completed, but his intercession for his people continues.

THE PRIEST JESUS

Jesus was a prophet on the earth. However, viewing Jesus as priest on the earth is not as common and is sometimes even contested. People typically consider Jesus a priest at the end of his life, as he offered his blood, but to view Jesus' entire life under the banner of priest is not as routine. This hesitation partially stems from Hebrews 8:4, where the author says, "Now if he were on earth, he would not be a priest at all, since there are priests who offer gifts according to the law."

A more expansive view of the Bible, however, proves that priesthood came long before the Levites. Adam, Abraham, and Moses were all priests in their own right. The task of the Levites matured in deeper soil. Hebrews affirms that Christ's priesthood stems from a different order from the Mosaic law—his comes from Melchizedek, which precedes Aaron's. We should therefore view Christ's priestly work like his prophetic and kingly work: Jesus was *designated* and acted as priest on the earth, but *installed* as the priest in heaven.[1] While Christ's work on the cross was central to his priestly work, rich indications persist of Jesus' priesthood in his ministry before his death.

Matthew begins by defining Jesus' name: "Yeshua" means "God will save his people from their sins" (Matt 1:21–23; see also Ezek 36:29; 37:23). The saving from sins is a distinctly priestly task. Jesus was labeled the mediator between God and humanity at the start of his life (1 Tim 2:5). The priesthood theme continued as Jesus was anointed at his baptism—already a descent/ascent pattern. Priests went through cleansing rituals before entering God's presence. In this ceremony, priests were ordained for their priestly service, and therefore we can rightly conclude Jesus' baptism ordained him to his human priestly role.[2]

In Jesus' baptism, God declared him to be the beloved Son with whom he was pleased (Luke 3:22). Calling him the beloved Son means God chose Jesus as his representative. Asserting God

---

1. From a systematic perspective, his prophetic, priestly, and kingly roles took place in eternal decree (*pactum salutis*).

2. Both kings and priests were anointed, and Psalm 110 shows that the kingly and priestly tasks should not be separated.

was pleased with him is akin to the pleasing aroma before God that the priests offered. Not surprisingly, then, Jesus began his ministry at the age of thirty (Luke 3:23). Priests also began their ministry at this age (Num 4:3, 23, 30, 35, 39, 43, 47; 1 Chr 23:3).

Jesus also instructed people how to approach God as priest when he taught them how to pray before their Father in the Lord's Prayer. In the Lord's Prayer, Jesus the priest invited them into the holy of holies with him and taught them how to approach the throne of grace. He told them to call out to God as "Our Father in Heaven." This is a priestly call, asking to approach the throne of God as sons of God. When Jesus told his disciples to ask for daily bread, this not only alluded to the exodus tradition, but also recalled the bread of presence given to priests (Lev 24:5–9).[3] In the Lord's Prayer, Jesus welcomed them into the throne room of God, telling them to call on God as Father.

Jesus' healing ministry also paints him as a priest. He healed those who bore leprosy, and Leviticus outlines how lepers were to go to priests to have their cleanliness evaluated (Lev 13–14). Jesus stretched out his arm and touched a leper, making him clean and sending him back into the congregation (Matt 8:1–4). In Mark 2, Jesus acted as a priest as he not only healed, but combined healing with the forgiveness of sins. Old-covenant priests could not include the crippled in God's temple, nor could they ultimately forgive sin, but Jesus completed both acts. Jesus also claimed authority over the Sabbath on multiple occasions and healed individuals on this important day. In so doing, Jesus declared he was the greater priest because "the priests in the temple profane the Sabbath and are guiltless" (Matt 12:5).

---

3. Nicholas Perrin, *Jesus the Priest* (Grand Rapids: Baker Academic, 2019), 17–53.

Jesus was not only a priest in his positive actions he acted as a subversive priest. Priests were to serve in the temple, but Jesus predicted the end of the temple period, leading to his crucifixion. When Jesus entered Jerusalem, he did not come to restore the temple; rather, he stormed into the temple, disrupting the selling and trading (Mark 11:15; Luke 19:45; John 2:15). In Matthew 24, Jesus climatically left the temple and predicted the temple would be destroyed (Matt 24:1-2; Mark 13:1-2; Luke 21:5-6). At his trial they accused him of saying he would destroy the temple and raise it in three days (Matt 26:61; 27:40; Mark 14:58; 15:29; John 2:19-21). John is the only Gospel writer to note Jesus spoke about the temple of his body. Jesus both condemned the current priestly system and fulfilled it by replacing it with his own body. His actions were destructive for the purpose of rebuilding.

Finally, Jesus died on the cross as both the sacrificial lamb and the priestly mediator. In all the Synoptics, when Jesus died, the temple curtain was torn in two (Matt 27:51; Mark 15:38; Luke 23:45). Earlier Jesus interpreted his death at the Last Supper through the bread (body) and wine (blood). Bread and blood were central to the priest's role. Hebrews interprets Jesus' death as Jesus offering his own blood and thus securing an eternal redemption (Heb 9:12-14). He mediated a better covenant as the true high priest (Heb 12:24). At the ascension, Jesus did not cease from acting in his priestly role; the locale simply shifted.

PORTRAIT OF A PRIEST

Priests had precise and definite roles in the Old Testament. Priests were essentially those who served God and God's people by mediating before God's altar, the place where heaven and earth met.[4]

---

4. David S. Schrock helpfully describes priests as "consecrated mediators who stand to serve at God's altar, (1) sanctifying God's holy place, (2) sacrificing God's offerings, (3) speaking God's covenant" (*The Royal Priesthood and the*

The author of Hebrews gives three descriptions of a priest (Heb 5:1): priests were chosen from among humanity, acted on behalf of humanity, and offered gifts and sacrifices to God.

First, priests were chosen from among humanity. They were *chosen* in that they were appointed by God. Israel was chosen by God to be a royal priesthood (Exod 19:6). Exodus 28:1 describes how the Lord brought Aaron to serve as priest. The Levites were exclusively appointed as a clan to serve as priests. As the author of Hebrews asserts: "No one takes this honor for himself, but only when called by God, just as Aaron was" (Heb 5:4). Priesthood was not claimed, demanded, or requested. God bestowed, bequeathed, and appointed priests.

Priests also had to be chosen *from humanity*. They had to be of flesh and blood—taken from among humankind. Animals, spirits, and angels could not be priests. A priest had to be human because humans are uniquely and distinctively made in the image of God and therefore can mediate this relationship between God and the people. Only a priest could image both people to God and God to people. Priesthood language is both exclusive and inclusive. Particular priests existed within Israel, but Adam is also portrayed as a priest, and Israel was called to be a "kingdom of priests" (Exod 19:6).

Second, priests acted on behalf of humanity. Though they served in various capacities, essentially priests attended or served in God's house *for* humanity. They maintained the edifice of the house of God on behalf of God's people. As they maintained this house for God, they entered God's presence representing, mediating, and interceding for God's people. The

---

Glory of God [Wheaton, IL: Crossway, forthcoming]). Schrock emphasizes priests' speaking and guarding role. My description is complementary, not contradictory, to his.

priests were those who *came near to the Lord* (Exod 19:22). Priests went before God with blood splattered on their garments and a breastplate of twelve jewels on their chest. The priest came before God covered in the death of another, or alternatively, with the life of another covering them.

Third, priests offered gifts and sacrifices. Offerings were the specific and exclusive actions priests performed *as* human beings *for the sake* of human beings but *before* God. Priests did not enter the presence of God without offerings: gifts and sacrifices. The first explicit priest mentioned in the Bible is Melchizedek, who brought out bread and wine to Abraham. Priests killed animals before the Lord and brought the blood before the Lord (Lev 1:5, 11, 15). They brought flour, oil, and grain and burned it as a memorial portion on the altar (Lev 2:2, 9). Priests were the ones to restore the altar (Ezra 3:1–7), celebrate the Passover (6:19–22), and offer evening sacrifices (9:4–5).

Behind all of these gifts and sacrifices stands the theological truth that God is holy and these offerings were a pleasing aroma to him that assuaged his anger against sin. Sin destroyed, but God looked to the sacrifices as repentant rituals. Something died, and its life was presented to God on behalf of violating the covenant. Priests therefore mediated and interceded for the people so that they might continue in the grace of God.

While the Old Testament celebrates the ministry of priests, indications of their insufficiency abound. All of their actions had a sense of incompleteness and inadequacy to them. Many of the priests in the Old Testament were corrupt and did what was expressly forbidden in the Torah. Neither Levites nor the nation could attain wholeness under that system (Heb 7:11). Priests in the Old Testament were still stained by sin (7:26), entered repeatedly with the blood of animals, and went into a man-made tent (9:7, 11, 25; 10:11). These sacrifices could never take away sins. It was impossible for the blood of animals to take away sins (10:4).

Adam, the Levites, and the nation of Israel as a whole were to act as priests on behalf of humanity, but they all failed in this task. God called Israel to be a kingdom of priests (Exod 19:6), but it did not retain the resolve or ability to complete this task. The Old Testament thus pushes readers forward to a greater coming priest.

SHADOW STORIES
OF THE PRIEST'S ASCENT

The Old Testament prepares readers with stories of priests who sacrificed, ascended the mountain of God, and then interceded and blessed the people. Jesus performed the actions of a priest while on earth. After his ascent this role did not cease, but shifted into its consummation in a unique way. Three ascension stories resound with themes pointing to a shift in Christ's priestly task. The change meant he became even a better priest.

MOSES ASCENDED MOUNT SINAI

The first story that foreshadows Christ's priestly ascent is Moses' ascent to Mount Sinai. In Exodus 24, God told Moses to come up on the mountain while the rest of Israel should worship from afar. "Moses alone shall come near to the LORD, but the others shall not come near, and the people shall not come up with him" (Exod 24:2). Moses rose early in the morning, built an altar, and offered burnt offerings and peace offerings to the Lord. He took blood and threw it against the altar and held forth the book of the covenant, binding Israel to what it had agreed on. He made a sacrifice before he ascended.

Then Moses went up on the mountain and met the God of Israel (Exod 24:10). The scene is portrayed as a heavenly vision as he sees sapphire stone. In the presence of God, they ate and drank, and a cloud covered the mountain as Moses met with God.

> So Moses rose with his assistant Joshua, and Moses went up into the mountain of God. And he said to the elders, "Wait here for us until we return to you." ... Then Moses went up on the mountain, and the cloud covered the mountain. The glory of the LORD dwelt on Mount Sinai, and the cloud covered it six days. And on the seventh day he called to Moses out of the midst of the cloud. Now the appearance of the glory of the LORD was like a devouring fire on the top of the mountain in the sight of the people of Israel. Moses entered the cloud and went up on the mountain. And Moses was on the mountain forty days and forty nights. (Exod 24:13-18)

On the mountain, Moses interceded for the people as their representative. He received God's law and spoke to God on behalf of the people and then came down from the mountain to speak to the people on behalf of God. Moses blessed the people, communicating to them God's presence. On the mountain, Moses received details about how they would build the tabernacle so that God might dwell with his people (Exod 25-31).

Moses' pattern pointed forward to the Levites' task but ultimately to Christ (sacrifice > ascent > intercession > blessing). Priests also sacrificed and ascended into the presence of God, and smoke and fire filled the room as they brought their blood offerings. They then interceded for the people and came forth and blessed the people.

As readers continue through the Old Testament, it becomes clear Moses' ascent was a type to be fulfilled. Moses did not stay up on the mountain, the tabernacle could be defiled, Moses' intercession ceased, and the people did not follow their covenant instructions.

THE HIGH PRIEST ENTERED THE HOLY OF HOLIES

A second account that foreshadows Christ's priestly ascension is the high priest entering the holy of holies (Lev 16:2–34). Though Leviticus can be confusing to modern readers with its focus on Jewish rituals, the narrative structure leads to the Day of Atonement (Yom Kippur), when the high priest ascended to meet God. Everything before this day taught people how they must approach the presence of God, and everything after this day instructed the people how they might dwell in the presence of God. Leviticus is thus a book about ascending the mountain of the Lord.[5] Like Moses, the high priest exclusively entered into the presence of God in a specific way so that he might intercede for the people of Israel.

Strict divisions existed in the tabernacle. A tent curtain divided the courtyard from the rest of the nation, another curtain divided the holy place from the courtyard, and a final curtain divided the most holy place from the holy place. The division of the spaces represented the cosmos. Priests entered into the highest heavens as they entered the holy of holies to meet with God and intercede for the people. Cherubim on the curtains indicated that they symbolically entered the heavens.

Aaron was commanded to come inside the veil in an ordered way, for the Lord would appear in the cloud over the mercy seat. The cloud kept him from beholding the full glory of the Lord. He came before the Lord with a sacrifice (Lev 16:3, 6–10, 25), dressed in a holy linen coat (16:4), bathed (16:4, 24), with incense before

---

5. L. Michael Morales, *Who Shall Ascend the Mountain of the Lord? A Biblical Theology of the Book of Leviticus* (Downers Grove, IL: InterVarsity Press, 2015).

the Lord (16:12–13), and with blood sprinkled seven times on the mercy seat and the altar (16:14, 19). Exodus 28:29 informs readers that when the high priest entered the holy place he bore the names of the sons of Israel on his breastpiece, thus indicating going before God on behalf of the people. The high priest mediated—a vicarious human acting on behalf of others.

The goal of going before God was to be in his presence, but the means was blood. The high priest had to make atonement. Two goats were offered. The first propitiated for the people's sin (Lev 16:15). The high priest took the blood from this first goat and spread it on the atonement cover of the ark as intercession before the Lord. When he emerged, the high priest placed his hands on the head of the second goat, the scapegoat. He confessed all the sins of the people, putting them on the goat, and then this goat was released into the wilderness. The second goat demonstrated how God had removed the sins of the people. Both teach that sins were forgiven and removed: propitiated and expiated.

Like the story of Moses ascending Mount Sinai, the high priestly ascent into the holy of holies foreshadows Christ's heavenly ascension. The high priest symbolically ascended the ladder of the cosmos by going past the veil and met with God in his house. Priests interceded and atoned for Israel in the presence of God as smoke and fire filled the holy of holies. Their actions prepared the way for Christ, who ascended once into the presence of God as the true High Priest. God chose his representatives, but his ultimate representative had to be clean, clothed, and covered in blood.

DAVID'S ASCENT OF THE LORD'S HILL

The final image that foreshadows Christ's priestly ascent comes from the lips of David in Psalm 24. Though David was a king, he also performed many priestly activities, thus presaging a

reuniting of these roles.[6] He asked for the priestly bread from
Ahimelech to sustain himself and his men in 1 Samuel 21. Later,
in 2 Samuel 6, David had the ark brought to Jerusalem and performed many priestly tasks: he offered sacrifices (vv. 13, 17),
wore an ephod (v. 14), erected a tabernacle (v. 17), and blessed
the people (v. 18). Then, in 2 Samuel 24, David sought favor
from God by interceding on behalf of the people. This came in
response to David's prideful census. The prophet Gad instructed
him to erect an altar to sacrifice and burn offerings on it. David
is therefore presented as a priest-king—one who brings these
two offices into union again.

It is no surprise, then, that David speaks as a priest in the
Psalms, asking who will ascend the mountain of the Lord. In
Psalm 24, David begins by confessing the whole earth is the
Lord's because he is its creator (Ps 24:1-2). God owns all, and
the priest mediates that sovereign blessing to the people. David
then asks a distinctly priestly question: "Who shall ascend the
hill of the LORD? And who shall stand in his holy place?" (Ps
24:3). Essentially, he asks who will receive God's favor and also
confer it to God's people.

His answer centers on cleanliness—a metaphor crowded with
priestly imagery. The one who can ascend has clean hands and
a pure heart. David affirms the one who ascends the mountain
of the Lord is the one who is clean both outwardly (hands) and
inwardly (heart). Entering before God's presence was not merely
a ritualistic act where outward actions could cleanse. God wanted
the whole person—inside and out—dedicated to his character.
Sacrifices were the means by which people became clean.

This theme is further emphasized as David asserts the one
who will enter into God's temple does not lift up his soul to what

---

6. See Perrin, *Jesus the Priest*, 153-54.

is false. The one who ascends is not an idolater; he does not worship other gods. God will only allow those who are faithful to him to come into his presence. They are not to seek to ascend to God through their own means like at Babel. Rather, they are to worship God and God alone. Finally, the one who ascends has a pure and clean mouth. He does not swear deceitfully. God's emphasis on living as a truthful person is based on his character. When he says something will occur, he makes sure it comes to pass. Only the one who imitates him as a truth teller shall stand in his holy place.

David's point is that the true priest will be clean—holistically pure and washed. He will not be an idolater, his inside life will match his outside, and his lips will be unpolluted. This person will receive blessings from the presence of the Lord—righteousness from his throne. David asks, "Who will ascend the mountain of the Lord?" Only those who have a sacrifice covering them can ascend and receive blessings from God.

The one who met this portrait would be endowed to ascend the mountain of the Lord. The Old Testament indicates that while David was a righteous man, no human being could achieve this because they were all stained with sin. They would try to ascend the mountain of God only to find themselves tumbling to the foot of the mountain. A new priest had to come who would be truly authorized to ascend the mountain of the Lord.

THE ASCENSION AND THE SACRIFICE, INTERCESSION, AND BLESSING OF THE PRIEST

The Old Testament gives instructions concerning the priestly cult, yet these were only shadows. In these images it became clear the priesthood was lacking—it could never make perfect. The priests served as flawed individuals for a flawed nation.

They sacrificed in tents and temples with the blood of animals. They came into service to intercede repeatedly for their own sins and the sins of the nation.

Therefore, when Jesus occupied the space of the earth, he did so as the true priest. He fulfilled what the priesthood lacked. Yet, it was not until Jesus ascended that he entered completely into his priestly role. Upon his entering into heaven, God *installed* him as an eternal high priest. Because of his perfect sacrifice, Jesus intercedes in a better way, and he blesses his people as the great High Priest with the peace of the Holy Spirit. While Jesus was also a better priest on the earth, the Messiah's ascension escalated and expanded his priestly work. He was a priest on the earth; now he acts as priest in heaven.

The Messiah's ascent thus did not put a stop to his priestly work; on the contrary, it transferred this role into a new epoch. Hebrews 4:14 affirms Jesus still acts as our priest in heaven. "Since we have a great high priest who has ascended into heaven, Jesus the Son of God, let us hold firmly to the faith we profess" (NIV). Though many avenues could be explored in regard to how Christ's priestly work shifted at the ascent, a few rise to the surface that can be put under the banner of *person*, *place*, and *action*.

1. Jesus ministers as a better priest in his person.

2. Jesus serves in a better place, the heavenly tent.

3. Jesus' better priestly actions (sacrificial presentation, intercession, and blessing) continue and are confirmed.

A HEAVENLY BODY (PERSON)

The author to the Hebrews argues Jesus entered uniquely into his priestly role after his resurrection and ascension. He did so because he was no longer merely an earthly priest, but a heavenly priest with a glorified body. The heavenly priesthood of Jesus must be affirmed from two different angles: Jesus as the heavenly priest still partakes of flesh, and he is the exalted and pure priest.

The Old Testament affirms priests had to be taken from among men (Heb 5:1), and the ascension continues Jesus' incarnation. Therefore Jesus remains as our priest because he is of flesh. Though the ascension must be thought of as beyond our notions of space and time, we must also think of the Messiah's ascent in relation to a permanent incarnation and actual relations of space and time. The ascent of Christ the priest was still the ascent of the *man* Christ. His ascension did not undo his humanity—it confirmed it.[7]

Enormous theological problems arise if we disembody the Messiah's ascension. For "if Jesus did not go up as a man, he cannot come again as a man," nor can Jesus serve as humanity's priest if he is not still of the flesh.[8] The ascension thus glorified Christ *in* his incarnation. To put this another way, Luke, in recounting the ascent, does not abandon history—he maintains that eschatology determines history. The Messiah's ascent becomes the culmination of Jesus' incarnation.

In this way, the ascent did not dissolve the importance of the physical existence of Jesus, nor the importance of the incarnation. Rather the ascension exalted and confirmed the incarnation. The ascension "is the setting of man, once and for all, within the open horizons of the trinitarian life and love," Farrow

---

7. Douglas Farrow, *Ascension and Ecclesia: On the Significance of the Doctrine of the Ascension for Ecclesiology and Christian Cosmology* (Grand Rapids: Eerdmans, 1999), 242.

8. Gerrit Scott Dawson, *Jesus Ascended: The Meaning of Christ's Continuing Incarnation* (New York: T&T Clark, 2004), 5.

writes.[9] Though Jesus has withdrawn from visible and physical contact with his people, Torrance says his ascension "sends us back to the historical Jesus as the covenanted place on earth and in time which God has appointed for meeting between man and himself."[10]

Jesus' continuing incarnation is one aspect of his priestly identity, but so is his purity and the exaltation of his body. Unlike the priests on earth, Jesus is holy, innocent, unstained, separated from sinners (Heb 7:26). He is the pure priest David spoke of who ascends the mountain of the Lord (Ps 24). Unlike the Old Testament priests who continually had to offer sacrifices both for their own sins and for the sins of the nation, Jesus is separate and unstained from sin.

Jesus is also different from other priests because he has been exalted to the heavens (Heb 7:26). Jesus is still a man—but he does not possess the same body he possessed on earth. He went up with his transformed body (Phil 3:21; 1 Cor 15). Jesus did not adorn himself with humanity to simply discard it. He adorned himself with humanity so that he might perfect humanity as our true priest.

In the Old Testament, priests were chosen among men to represent humankind before God. They entered into the cloud of incense because they couldn't bear to view the glory of God. Now Christ serves as the better priest at the right hand of God with his glorified body. Only the transformed body can behold the true glory of God and not be destroyed. That is why Jesus said to his disciples, "Where I am going, you cannot come" (John 8:21–22; 13:33). Our bodies have not been made new, nor have we

9. Douglas Farrow, *Ascension Theology* (New York: Bloomsbury, 2013), 36.

10. Thomas F. Torrance, *Atonement: The Person and Work of Christ*, ed. Robert T. Walker (Downers Grove, IL: IVP Academic, 2014), 292.

conquered death like Jesus. Only Jesus can now intercede forever and eternally because Jesus is our enduring, exalted, and pure priest.

Christ therefore is the true priest because he is the God-Man who represents humanity as the firstfruits of those who will dwell with God forever. He is not like the priests of the earth, who interceded through the weakness of their flesh and only came occasionally. He ministers continually and serves in the power of the resurrection.

A HEAVENLY TENT (PLACE)

Not only does Jesus minister as a better priest after the ascent because he has been granted a better body, but he serves in a better place. "The ascension is not merely removal *from* a place, but also *to* a place," Farrow writes.[11] Heaven is really a place, yet it is also beyond what we can refer to in human terms. It cannot be located on any map of ours, as the place he resides extends through all time and places. When Jesus went to heaven, he moved from the old creation to the new creation.[12] Heaven is the dwelling place of God—the control room for the universe.

The Old Testament provides a dizzying amount of detail concerning the structure of the tabernacle. Both the Old Testament authors and the writer to the Hebrews considered these details important—but also contend they point to something greater. Temple and tabernacle divisions represented the cosmos. The tabernacle was thus the cosmos in miniature and functioned as an image of ascent into God's presence. The most holy place corresponded to the highest heavens, where God dwelt; the holy

---

11. Farrow, *Ascension Theology*, 45.

12. This paragraph is dependent on Farrow, *Ascension Theology*, 43–49.

place matched the heavens (or sky); the courtyard was Israel's land; and outside the courtyard was the world and sea.

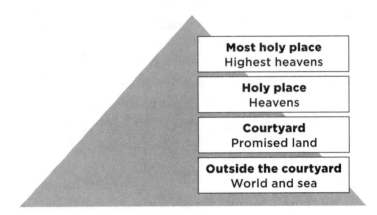

| **Most holy place** |
| Highest heavens |
| **Holy place** |
| Heavens |
| **Courtyard** |
| Promised land |
| **Outside the courtyard** |
| World and sea |

At the ascension Jesus began to minister in the actual highest heavens. The most holy place symbolized the reality Jesus now fulfills at his ascent. Priests offered their sacrifices on earth, but Jesus now offers his blood in the true tent. Twice the author to the Hebrews speaks of Jesus as a minister in "the true tent" (Heb 8:2) or a "more perfect tent" (9:11).

In both of these texts the heavenly tent is better because the Lord has made it: it is "the true tent that the Lord set up, not man" (8:2), and the tent is "not made with hands, that is, not of this creation" (9:11). "Handmade" in the Scriptures refers to the old creation, while "made without hands" refers to the new creation (Dan 2:34, 45; Mark 14:58; Acts 17:24; Heb 9:11, 24).[13] The point is not that the earthly tabernacle or temple was necessarily defective; they were temporary. God built the highest heavens.

---

13. At other times "made with hands" refers to idolatry. The theme reaches all the way back to the story of Babel, where the people tried to make a way to God through their own hands (Gen 11:1-9).

Heaven "is absolutely different from earth and higher and as such in antithesis to it," as Karl Barth writes.[14] Priests entered what was symbolic for the highest heavens; Jesus entered the highest heavens.

Jesus fulfilled his priestly role at the ascent in a unique way because he now ministers in the true tent—the heavenly tent—but he also does so as the true man. The high priest entered before God and would only get a glimpse of the new creation, but now Jesus ministers in the place God himself has made.

A HEAVENLY PRESENTATION (ACTION 1)

While we have a better priest (person) and better tent (place), priests were chiefly defined by their *actions*. Priests were taken from among men, but appointed *to act* on behalf of humanity by offering gifts and sacrifices. High priests chiefly offered sacrifices for the people on the Day of Atonement.

Priests in the Old Testament went behind the curtain to bring Israel with them. They entered because of the sacrifice they offered. In the same way, Jesus' intercession is based on his sacrificial work on the cross. One aspect of Jesus' priestly service includes intercession—but intercession does not exist unaccompanied. As with Moses, the Levites, and David, ascending and interceding only happens after sacrifice. Intercession therefore is built on a more foundational reality: sacrifice. Atonement is the groundwork on which intercession stands.

Jesus does not sacrifice himself again in heaven; rather, he *presents* the blood already sacrificed.[15] His death was a single

---

14. Karl Barth, *Church Dogmatics* (Edinburgh: T&T Clark, 1932–1967), IV.15.2, 153.

15. Donne states the sacrifice is over, but *the sacrifice* forever remains. Brian Donne, *Christ Ascended: A Study in the Significance of the Ascension of Jesus Christ in the New Testament* (Exeter, UK: Paternoster, 1983), 37. Swete affirms something similar: "Heaven is not a place of sacrifice, and our Lord is no longer a

offering (Heb 7:27; 9:28; 10:12, 14). He enters into the throne room, behind the veil, with his bloodstained body. Priests in the Old Testament came into the presence of God with blood splattered on the curtains, their robes, and bodies. In the same way, Jesus comes covered in blood before the Father, thereby completing his act of atonement. In this manner, the ascension does not move past the cross but puts the cross ever before our eyes.[16] By faith we too look up and see Christ's sacrifice for us.

Christ's sacrificial presentation therefore restores the broken covenant between God and humanity, and creates an intimate union between God and his people. We enjoy the benefits of the Father's love and presence as Jesus does in heaven because we are united to Jesus. Torrance writes, "Christ was once and for all sacrificed in our stead on the Cross but he has ascended into the Holy Place and ever lives to present Himself (and us *in Him* because of Himself *for us*) before the face of the Father."[17]

If Jesus were to leave heaven, then the pledge of our salvation would be removed. If Jesus is not in God's presence on our behalf, then we are not in God's presence. Our presence before God is Christ's presence before God. To put this more pointedly, without the Messiah's ascent, we are not in the covenantal presence of God. The ascent is good news because Jesus intercedes for his people at the right hand of God and even brings us with him on his breastplate before the Father.

Sacrificing Priest; he has offered one sacrifice for sins forever. But his presence in the Holiest is a perpetual and effective presentation before God of the sacrifice once offered." H. B. Swete, *The Ascended Christ: A Study in the Earliest Christian Teaching* (London: Macmillan, 1911), 43.

16. William Milligan, *The Ascension and Heavenly Priesthood of Our Lord* (Eugene, OR: Wipf & Stock, 2006), 143.

17. Thomas F. Torrance, *Royal Priesthood: A Theology of Ordained Ministry* (Edinburgh: T&T Clark, 2003), 14–15, 17.

A HEAVENLY INTERCESSION (ACTION 2)

At the ascent, Jesus' priestly activity on behalf of humanity did not cease but entered into a new era. The Messiah's ascension allowed him to intercede on behalf of humanity in a unique way. Though it is tempting to view Jesus' sitting at the right hand of God as the completion of his work, this is only partially true (Heb 1:3). Jesus did not ascend into the heavens to merely sit and rest. He did not soar into the sky because his intercessory work had concluded. Even in his sitting he continues to serve.

Hebrews 8:1–2 affirms this reality.

> Now the main point of what we are saying is this: We do have such a high priest, who sat down at the right hand of the throne of the Majesty in heaven, and *who serves in the sanctuary*, the true tabernacle set up by the Lord, not by a mere human being. (NIV)

Hebrews couples Jesus' sitting with serving. We enjoy a high priest who still works in the heavens. His vocation is not finished, but it is based on his accomplished sacrifice. He serves in the heavenly sanctuary as the Levites served on the earth. Hebrews 7:25 affirms Christ always lives to make intercession for believers. Romans 8:34 states Christ "is at the right hand of God, who indeed is interceding for us." This intercession is usually understood in the form of petitions. He pleads on behalf of his people, and the Father always hears him. The prayers of our Lord are thus continual and unceasing on our behalf.

Previously, I emphasized how Jesus sent us the Helper or Advocate—the Holy Spirit (John 14:16). However, in the Scriptures there are two advocates. Jesus Christ is also our advocate with the Father (1 John 2:1). We therefore retain both an external (Jesus Christ) and internal (Holy Spirit) advocate.[18] One advocates for us in heaven, the other from the earth. The Son advocates *with* the Father, while the Spirit *transfers* these benefits to our being.

Jesus advocates and intercedes on our behalf. He is our petitioner in heaven. In Hebrews 2:11–13 we read more of what this lobbying looks like. Jesus says he voices our names; in the midst of the congregation he sings the praises of his people. Jesus unashamedly calls us brothers. At the right hand of the Father he tells God of the people he has ransomed. He shows God the twelve stones on his chest and advocates for them. He says, "Here I am, and the children God has given me" (Heb 2:13 NIV).

This is a remarkable truth. At Jesus' ascent, he sits at the right hand of the Father and advocates, mediates, and intercedes on behalf of his people. Jesus is not embarrassed by his people. He proudly represents his people as the God-Man before the Father. Like the priests of old, he wears you as jewels on his breastplate.

A HEAVENLY BLESSING (ACTION 3)

Priests essentially served before God: they interceded based on their sacrifices. Yet, priestly intercession had a goal: receiving blessings from the face of God and distributing that blessing to God's people. In the Old Testament, as the high priest left the tent of meeting he lifted up his hands and blessed the people (Lev 9:22–23). This was modeled after both Moses and Melchizedek, who blessed Israel and Abraham. Numbers provides the content of the priestly blessing: "The LORD bless you and keep you; the LORD make his face to shine upon you and be gracious to you; the LORD lift up his countenance upon you and give you peace" (Num 6:24–26).

---

18. Milligan, *Ascension and Heavenly Priesthood*, 159.

Jesus blesses us in a similar way as our high priest. Right before Jesus ascended in Luke, he lifted up his hands and blessed his people (Luke 24:50–51). In Luke, God's blessing is regularly connected with his presence (Luke 1:42, 68–69; 2:28–32). Acts recounts that this blessing includes the Holy Spirit, and John 14:26–27 connects the gift of the Spirit with the high priest's blessing in Numbers. Jesus affirmed that the Helper would teach the disciples all things. More specifically, Jesus identified this teaching as, "Peace I leave with you; my peace I give to you" (John 14:27).

Jesus, as the great High Priest, is the new Aaron who extends his hands over the people and gives them peace through the Holy Spirit; his priestly blessing gifts the Spirit—the one who allows peace. Jesus not only gives the Aaronic blessing but fulfills it.[19] "The great High Priest came and not only pronounced the benediction, but he *became the benediction*," as Kelly Kapic puts it.[20]

Torrance correctly connects the blessing with Pentecost: "Pentecost is the content and actualization of that high priestly blessing. He ascended in order to fill all things with his presence and bestow gifts of the Spirit upon men."[21] The timing of the gift of the Spirit is important here. Only *after* Jesus ascended was he positioned to give his people the Spirit as the priest. The Messiah's ascension marks the perfection of his work as priest. Some Puritans therefore spoke of the ascension in terms of

---

19. Kapic says, "Whereas Aaron could lift his arms and pray for God's face to shine on the people, in seeing Jesus ascending into the heavens these believers saw the actual face of God shining. While they had heard of God's graciousness, now they had seen him who is Gracious. While they had held out for God's lifted countenance, they now saw it actualized." Kelly M. Kapic, "Receiving Christ's Priestly Benediction: A Biblical, Historical, and Theological Exploration of Luke 24:50–53," *Westminster Theological Journal* 67, no. 2 (2005): 252.

20. Kapic, "Receiving Christ's Priestly Benediction," 252.

21. Thomas F. Torrance, *Space, Time and Resurrection* (New York: T&T Clark, 2000), 118.

military triumph corresponding to Roman triumphs. He demonstrated his victory both positively and negatively: he bound his enemies (sin, death, and Satan), and then distributed gifts (the Holy Spirit and officers of the church).[22] When Jesus ascended to the right hand of the Father, he blessed his people with the Holy Spirit, washing them and making them clean (Rev 1:5–6).

The Spirit therefore became the link between believers and the Godhead. Through the Spirit those who have faith in Christ are filled with God as the Spirit indwells them. "But he who is joined to the Lord becomes one spirit with him" (1 Cor 6:17). As Jesus cries "Abba, Father," so the church now cries through the Spirit "Abba, Father." The same peace Jesus had with the Father he now bestows on us. The same joy he had through the Spirit, he now gives to us. The same light that emanated from Jesus now emanates from us.

The blessing of Spirit, through the priestly work of Christ, allows us to draw near to the Father. The Messiah's ascension marked the Aaronic bestowing of the Spirit on his followers. We now stand in the presence of God by the gift of the Spirit, who gives us peace with God.

CONCLUSION

Christ's priesthood on the earth was a glorious reality. He was anointed, he healed, he interceded, he blessed, and he cleansed his people by blood. However, we should also think of his priestly work as continuing and even entering a better era when he ascended into heaven. The ascension marks an important turn and shift in Christ's priestly work. To flatten or compress Christ's priestly work goes against the grain of scriptural progression.

---

22. Kapic, "Receiving Christ's Priestly Benediction," 259.

After Jesus' ascent and session, he undertook his role as the heavenly priest who interceded with his glorified body. After Jesus' ascent, he began to minister in the true tent in heaven. After Jesus' ascent, he began to serve in the sanctuary by interceding on our behalf and even presenting his blood before the Father, as priests would do in the Old Testament. Finally, only after Jesus' ascent did he bless his followers on earth like Aaron by pouring out the Holy Spirit.

Category	Priestly Work on Earth	Priestly Work in Heaven
Person	Earthly body, cleansed from sin	Spiritual body, unstained from sin
Place	Earthly tent	Heavenly tent

Action/Service

Sacrifice	Sacrificed himself and offered his blood	Presents his blood
Intercession	Interceded for his people on earth based on his sacrifice	Prays and renews covenant before the Father in heaven
Blessing	Gave his people peace through his words and actions	Bestows the Spirit, who gives his people access to God, peace, and confidence to draw near to God

The Aaronic blessing brings a point of transition. Christ's priestly work of pouring out the Spirit became the basis for the church being called a "kingdom of priests" and "living stones." Though Israel was called to this task, not until the Spirit came

were God's people given power to do so. In the act of granting
the Spirit, Christ made the church priests, and it became the
temple that is filled with the presence of God.

THE CHURCH AS PRIESTS

The church carries the mantle of prophet *and* priest. If Christ
fulfills the office of priesthood, then so does the church through
the power of the Spirit. The head cannot be separated from its
members. Christ lives in the church, and the church lives in him;
he indwells it, and it dwells with him.

This is why the church can be described as a kingdom of
priests and living stones (1 Pet 2:5, 9), because it has been built on
the cornerstone (1 Pet 2:4-8). As Jesus was the temple—the place
where God dwelt—so now through the Spirit Jews and gentiles
together become the place where God dwells. Paul in Ephesians
affirms that those in Christ are members of the household of
God, built on Christ Jesus, and growing into a holy temple (Eph
2:19-21). We are built together into a dwelling place for God *by
the Spirit* (Eph 2:22).

Throughout the Epistles the construction language of being
"built up" is ubiquitous. The apostles call the church to perform
priestly tasks that erect the temple. Paul can therefore say love
builds up (1 Cor 8:1), prophecy builds up (1 Cor 14:4), equipping
the saints for the ministry builds up (Eph 4:12), gracious speech
builds up (Eph 4:29), and encouragement builds up (1 Thess 5:11).

Not only is the church the built-up temple, but it fulfills
Israel's role—a kingdom of priests to the world. Jesus Christ,
the firstborn of the dead, has made his assembly a kingdom,
priests to his God and Father (Rev 1:5-6; 5:10; 20:6). The church
is a royal priesthood, made to proclaim the excellencies of our
great High Priest (1 Pet 2:9). The church therefore acts as priests,
mediating the presence of God to the earth because collectively

it is God's temple on the earth. The rest of the New Testament fills out the picture of how the church can act as priests on the earth because Christ is in heaven.

First, it does so by *self-sacrifice* and *offering*. Old Testament priests sacrificed animals before the Lord, but their life was also dedicated to service before God. They did not receive land like the rest of the tribes, and their life was sacrificed to serving before God. However, the ultimate example of self-sacrifice came in Christ, who offered himself on behalf of his people. Christ's offering compels our continual offerings. "Through him then let us continually offer up a sacrifice of praise to God, that is, the fruit of lips that acknowledge his name" (Heb 13:15; see Eph 5:2). We are to offer spiritual sacrifices (1 Pet 2:5), acceptable worship (Heb 12:28), and even our lives as drink offerings (Phil 2:17; 2 Tim 4:6).

In a similar way, for the church to be priests on the earth means Christians are to present their bodies as living sacrifices to God (Rom 12:1). They are to take up their crosses and follow Jesus unto death, renouncing all their rights. Paul in Ephesians specifically ties Christ's sacrifice as the model for us to walk in love (Eph 5:2). This means putting all bitterness, wrath, and slander away from us. It means being kind to one another, forgiving one another (Eph 4:31-32). Self-sacrifice means putting others' interests before one's own. As Christ emptied himself on the cross, now the church is called to do so as well.

Second, the church acts as priests on the earth by *intercession*. Paul constantly prays for his churches (Rom 1:10; 10:1; Eph 1:16; Phil 1:4; Col 1:3; 1 Thess 1:2; 2 Thess 1:11; Phlm 4-6) and asks that they pray for him (Rom 15:30; 2 Cor 1:11; Phil 1:19; Col 4:3; 1 Thess 5:25; 2 Thess 3:1). Paul commands those in Ephesus to pray "at all times in the Spirit, with all prayer and supplication" (Eph 6:18). Intercession for the body is part of the church's priestly task.

However, the church not only intercedes for those in the church, but prays for those who persecute it (Matt 5:44). Christians are to intercede for all people: for kings and for those who are in high positions (1 Tim 2:1–2). Members of the church lift their holy hands as priests to the world and intercede on behalf of the world. They mediate or plead that the presence of God would fill the world as the waters cover the sea. As Christ intercedes for his people, his people in turn intercede for the world. In the Old Testament the glory of the Lord filled the temple, and now the church prays that his presence would fill the whole earth.

Third, the church acts as priests on the earth by *instructing and declaring how people can draw near to God.* In this way members of the church act as Aaron blessing the world. The body points to the head and recognizes its source of life only comes from the head. Clerics on earth therefore point away from themselves and toward the priest Jesus, who grants access to God because he is in the presence of God. They instruct others that only through the ascended priest can people draw near with confidence (Heb 4:16). Only because he always makes intercession can the world have an advocate with God (1 John 2:1). Access to grace is obtained only through Christ (Rom 5:2), for only through him Jews and gentiles alike have access in one Spirit to the Father (Eph 2:18).

As priests, the church points to the High Priest. It looks to his breastplate and knows it is represented in heaven with him. The church looks not to itself but to the great High Priest who serves in heaven, the world's only hope of union with God forever.

CONCLUSION

At the ascension, Jesus uniquely fulfilled but also resumed his service as our priest. Divine appointment marks his priesthood.

He did not glorify himself to this role of priest, nor did humanity offer this to him. Rather the Lord appointed him as the priest: "You are my Son, today I have begotten you" (Ps 2:7; Heb 1:5; 5:5).

Though Jesus is a priest because he is human, he is also the glorified holy man, innocent, separated from sinners, and exalted above the heavens. Therefore, after the ascension he acts as our heavenly priest with a heavenly body who ministers in the heavenly tent. His economy stems not from the line of Aaron but from the line of Melchizedek, and therefore his priesthood endures forever.

As the priest, Jesus' actions and service also continue. He intercedes for his people and presents his blood before God the Father. He blesses his people as Aaron did. However, Jesus blesses his people with the gift of the Spirit. The Spirit advocates for us on earth; Christ advocates for us in heaven.

The Messiah's ascension was good news for his priestly office; the event cannot be sidelined, nor overlooked. It marks a shift in Christ's priestly work. Now his priestly work is universal, not limited to Israel. It is everlasting, never ceasing. It is unchangeable, never being superseded. It is effective, never dealing only outwardly with sin. It is pure, not stained by sin. It is heavenly, not relegated to the earth.

Rejoice, for Christ is our heavenly high priest forever.

CHAPTER 4

ASCENSION OF THE KING

Reigning over All

> *Your throne ... is forever and ever, the scepter of*
> *uprightness is the scepter of your kingdom.*
> *—Hebrews 1:8*

DECLARED LORD

The Lion King tells the story of a king's ascent. From the moment
the movie begins, Simba is branded as the heir to the throne. He
is *designated* to the office at the start of the movie by the baboon
Rafiki, who lifts up Simba before the animals of the kingdom as
they bow before him. He is the future king.

The rest of the story describes Simba's exile and his home-
coming to Pride Rock. When Simba returns to Pride Rock, he
must battle for the throne, which has been seized by his uncle
Scar. Simba conquers Scar and the hyenas, but even though he

has been designated, appointed, and even conquered the forces of darkness, his work remains incomplete.

At the end of the movie, immediately after the battle, an important scene occurs that is sometimes overlooked. The camera suddenly shifts to Rafiki, bringing the story full circle. Rafiki takes his staff and points Simba to Pride Rock. An old era has ended; a new one is about to begin.

In order for Simba to claim his kingdom and be installed as the king, he must ascend Pride Rock, the rightful place of the ruler, to ritually demonstrate he has conquered. Simba dramatically ascends the rock and roars. When he does, the other lions acknowledge his victory, dominion, and authority. Though Simba has been designated as the king from the start of the movie, though he has conquered in battle, he still is not installed as king until he ascends Pride Rock.

In a better way, Jesus is *designated* as the king and Lord from the beginning of the Gospels. God declared him to be David's son and anointed him as God's Son in the baptism. Jesus' mission on the earth was to defeat the powers of darkness, pay for sin, and restore the right rule of his kingdom. However, if readers stop after his victory, the story is left incomplete.

Jesus had to be *installed* as king; he had to be enthroned; he had to be recognized as king; he had to ascend to the right hand of the Father, sit on the throne, and receive from him all dominion and authority. Jesus did not simply come to the earth to conquer. He ascended to the right hand of the Father to receive his rightful rule. In doing this, his work as king culminates and continues. Kings sit down and are installed in order to rule. Jesus acted as a king on the earth; now he reigns as the king in heaven. The ascension is about the triumph of the king.

Though I have argued in each chapter that Christ's ascent shifted but also sustained Christ's threefold office, this chapter is unique. While all of the offices are of one piece, kingship is a primary metaphor, and therefore Christ's kingship stands at the pinnacle. To put this another way, the other offices flow from kingship and this office encompasses the others. Heppe comments that while kingship is historically last, it "comes first as the purpose of the other two offices."[1]

Kings ruled but also functioned in priestly and prophetic roles. They interceded for the nation and spoke the word of the Lord to the nation. The water did not flow the other direction. Prophets and priests did not rule like kings. Prophets declared the sovereign rule of God, and priests met with the true King. As Torrance asserts, "The priesthood of Christ is a Royal Priesthood, and the proclamation of Christ is a Royal Proclamation."[2] Thus, kingship is the root metaphor and provides the most momentous implications for Christ's ascension.

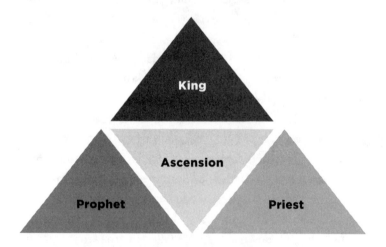

---

1. Heinrich Heppe, *Reformed Dogmatics*, trans. G.T. Thompson (Grand Rapids: Baker, 1978), 453.

2. T. F. Torrance, *Space, Time and Resurrection* (Grand Rapids: Eerdmans, 1976), 107.

THE LORD JESUS

Jesus arrived on the earth as the king. Though those in the first century labeled him a prophet, and though his actions were priestly, the Gospel writers are clear in their conviction that Jesus is the king Israel long waited for. The evangelists describe his birth in scarlet, and even Jesus' actions and words were kingly. Climactically, the story of his passion contains many royal resonances.

All the Gospel writers label Jesus as king, though at times this attribution is indirect. Matthew begins before Jesus' birth, proclaiming Jesus was the son of David (1:1). He hailed from the monarchial line promised it would always retain a son to sit on the throne (2 Sam 7). When Jesus was born, wise men came from the east and asked, "Where is he who has been born king of the Jews?" (Matt 2:2).

When Jesus began his ministry, his words were dipped in royalty. The summary of Jesus' message concerned the kingdom (Matt 4:17; Mark 1:15; Luke 4:43; John 18:36). Jesus constantly pointed his disciples toward the kingdom, called people into the kingdom, spoke of the future coming kingdom, and provided parables that explained the nature of the kingdom (Matt 13; Mark 4). Jesus compared and contrasted the nature of his kingship and kingdom with the tyranny of earthly kings (Luke 22:25). When he came into Jerusalem, Matthew asserts this fulfilled Zechariah, who spoke of Israel's king coming to them on a donkey (Matt 21:5). Multiple individuals also called out to Jesus in the Gospels as the son of David (Matt 9:27; 12:23; 15:22; 20:30–31; 21:9; 22:42; Mark 10:47–48; Luke 18:38–39).

Kings were called not only to meditate and teach the Torah so that the nation would flourish, but to embody the Torah as an example to their citizens (Deut 17:18–20). If they did so, the nation would be blessed. Jesus appeared proclaiming the gospel of the kingdom *and* healing every disease and affliction among the people (Matt 4:23). He taught on the Torah (Matt 5–7) and also embodied these actions in his life. Jesus was the wise king, the one who became the "living law."

When Jesus taught on a topic, Matthew especially emphasizes Jesus performed it as well. Jesus taught his disciples to be meek (5:5), and Matthew describes him as meek and lowly of heart (11:29; 21:5). Jesus called them to not neglect justice, mercy, and faithfulness (9:13; 12:7); he went about as king and willingly touched a leper, a hemorrhaging woman, and a girl believed to be dead in the house of a gentile (Matt 8–9). Jesus told his disciples to turn the other cheek when someone struck them (5:39), and in the trials Jesus allowed others to spit in his face and strike him (26:67; 27:30). As the true king, Jesus not only taught the law but embodied it.

Scarlet satire also fills the passion scene. Jesus was questioned as to whether he was the "King of the Jews" (Matt 27:11; Mark 15:2; Luke 23:3; John 18:33). The soldiers stripped Jesus and put a scarlet robe around him (Matt 27:28; Mark 15:17; John 19:2). They placed a crown of thorns on his head and a reed in his right hand as they mocked him and said, "Hail, King of the Jews!" (Matt 27:29; Mark 15:17–18; John 19:2–5; see Ps 89:39). With the reed, which functioned as a fake scepter, they struck him (Matt 27:29–30; Mark 15:19; Ps 2:9). The soldiers crowned him as king and then stripped him of his kingship.

The *titulus* became the final ironic proclamation of Jesus' kingship. Interestingly, none of the Gospels agree on the exact wording of the title, but they all declare Jesus was the king of the Jews (Matt 27:37; Mark 15:26; Luke 23:38; John 19:19). Jesus was crucified on the allegation of kingship. The Romans thus declared to the world why this man was crucified, but in a sardonic twist, the Gospel writers pronounce to their readers that the king has been enthroned. The sign (written in Aramaic, Latin, and Greek) declared to the whole known world that Jesus was *the king*.

In sum, the Gospels witness to the reality that Jesus came as the king. His mission was to set up his kingdom on the earth, but he did so through suffering and death. Through this sacrificial act he conquered the forces of darkness, forgave the sins of his people, and left an example for them to follow. Like the previous points, though, his kingship needs to be extended further than his life and death. The Messiah's ascent became a key piece of this monarchial montage.

PORTRAIT OF A KING

Though no sanctioned kings existed in Israel until the time after the judges, the concept precedes Saul and David.[3] When the time came for Israel to anoint an official king, a few qualifications, rights, and duties arose for this commission: kings were chosen by the Lord to rule with justice and righteousness, defeat Israel's enemies, promote the Torah, and bless the world. In all these descriptions, the Old Testament displays how each king of Israel lacked the strength and righteousness to accomplish these tasks. Therefore, with each portrayal a longing exists for a new and true king.

---

3. God, from the beginning, is understood to be the true King of the universe. Psalm 93:1–2 says, "The LORD reigns; he is robed in majesty. ... Your throne is established from of old; you are from everlasting." In Psalm 47:2, the Lord is called "a great King over all the earth." However, God also chose to exercise his kingship through both his agent and his agents. Adam, Eve, Abraham, and Israel were all to be kings and queens of the earth. Abraham is cast as a kingly figure (Gen 12:2–3; 17:2, 6, 8, 16; 22:18). He bore royal descendants ("Kings shall come from you," Gen 17:6). God promised to make Abraham into a great nation, to bless him, and to make his name great so that he would be a blessing (Gen 12:2). These are all king and kingdom promises.

First, kings were chosen by the Lord—they were his sons, his representatives. Deuteronomy 17:15 says Israel's king was to be "whom the LORD your God will choose." The king was to be an Israelite, but God would be the one to select their kings. This reality played itself out in the triad of kings who inaugurated the monarchial period. Saul was anointed (or chosen) by God's prophet Samuel (1 Sam 9:17; 10:1). The same ritual occurred for both David (1 Sam 16:13) and Solomon (1 Kgs 1:39). Kings in Israel did not claim this right for themselves; they were appointed by God himself and through his heralds.

Second, kings were essentially called to rule. They were to be God's agents who mediated his orders over the earth. The king was to rule with justice and righteousness. In Psalm 72 Solomon asks for justice and righteousness to judge the people. Kings were not to acquire possessions for themselves: horses, wives, or gold (Deut 17:16–17). They were not to take men and women for service, nor the land for themselves (1 Sam 8:10–18). The king's rule also included defeating enemies. Kings were to defend the nation. When Saul heard of the plight of those in Jabesh, he summoned the people and struck down the Ammonites (1 Sam 11:5–11). After this the people made Saul king (11:15), and the narrator indicates this was the commencement of his kingship. The same warrior mentality marked David's kingship as he conquered many around him.

Third, kings were to follow, delight in, and promote the Torah. The way to rule with justice and righteousness was by writing a copy of the law and reading it all the days of the king's life. The purpose was so that he would be a wise king—one who feared God (the true King) and kept all the commands (Deut 17:18–19). When David's time of death arrived, he pulled Solomon close to him and told him as the king he was to "keep the charge of the LORD your God, walking in his ways and keeping his statutes, his commandments, his rules, and his testimonies, as it is written in the Law of Moses" (1 Kgs 2:3). Josiah's reform came by reading the newly discovered Torah and declaring restoration (2 Kgs 22–23).

Finally, kings were to bless both the nation and the world through the wisdom, justice, and authority they had received from God. Abraham was given a blessing so that he would be a blessing (Gen 12:2). Blessings were never meant to be hoarded, locked up, or selfishly stored. God blessed kings so that they could extend this blessing. Psalm 72 reflects on this reality as the king provided for people. The king was like rain that fell on the grass, delivered the needy, and provided food. After Solomon built the temple, he turned around and blessed the assembly of Israel (1 Kgs 8:14). In this way, the king mediated the presence of God to the people of Israel.

All of the above are idealized portraits. None of the kings of Israel lived up to these requirements. In the dark days of Israel, kings began to appoint themselves and murder to attain this position. They acquired horses and wives and relied on their own strength or even the strength of other gods. Kings of Israel typically ruled for selfish purposes rather than righteous ones. Samuel warned the people the king would take their sons, daughters, land, food, and flock (1 Sam 8:10–18). Not only that, but Israel would be overthrown by the surrounding nations. The kings of Israel (both north and south) followed other gods and forgot the Torah. In all this, the kings did not bless Israel, nor the world.

The Old Testament thus sets the stage for a new coming king who will fulfill all these roles. Jesus' kingship was not fully manifest until he sat down at the right hand of the Father, and it will be most fully manifest when he returns. The Messiah's ascension marks the enthronement of the king after he had died for his people and fought their battle. Now he would rule in a new way in all righteousness and justice.

SHADOW STORIES
OF THE KING'S ASCENT

The Old Testament not only speaks of the duties and rights of the king, but foreshadows a future coming king who will ascend to God and sit down. Some of the most important texts in the Old Testament speak of a coming Israelite king who will ascend to rule the world. The Messiah's ascent is foreshadowed in Psalms 2; 110; and Daniel 7.

These particular texts carry a centralizing and climactic positioning in the Scriptures. The people of Israel were waiting for the triumph of their king. They anticipated the day when their ruler would be installed and coronated above all other kings. They expected the age when their king would defeat their enemies, rule in justice and righteousness, meditate on the Torah, and bless Israel and thereby the whole world. Critical texts told of this day—but the people had to wait. The ascension was therefore predicted long ago. It was central to the hopes of the Jews.

In Luke's literature the ascension is viewed from an earthly perspective, but these Old Testament texts fill out what happens in heaven. They peek behind the curtain and foretell the ascent and session of Christ. When Jesus ascended, these important texts came to life.

ADAM AND EVE'S DESCENT

Jesus' kingly ascent had to transpire because the biblical story begins with a tragic descent. Adam and Eve were created on the mountain garden of Eden. They were made to be the royal family, to rule the earth and bring order as God has done. Their monarchial role is made explicit when the text says Adam and Eve were created in the image and likeness of God. The idea of image and likeness communicates two main ideas: kingship and sonship.

In the ancient world, kings represented the image of God; they ruled on behalf of the gods. These ancient kings were characterized as images of the gods, and as living images they maintained or destroyed cosmic harmony. In the garden, Adam and Eve rebelled against their king and tried to snatch power for themselves. God therefore made them descend from the mountain to struggle and toil in their royal task.

The entire biblical story is therefore set up in terms of spatial movement. As kings and queens, humanity fell from the mountain of God. The resolution to this story had to come in someone ascending to God himself. If descent was the result of sin, then ascent was the solution.

The rest of the scriptural story line tells of how humanity continued to attempt to ascend to God but could not do so on their own. They were enslaved to the elements of the world, and someone had to ascend above to free them. They attempted to build cities (Babel), to exalt themselves above the heavens, to ignore God, but what they found was these actions only furthered their descent. The Bible thus prepares the way for a coming one who will ascend, restore, and even increase the fellowship and dominion humanity once possessed. Key Old Testament texts foreshadow this event in visions, poems, and songs.

PSALM 2 AND THE ASCENT OF THE KING

Psalm 1 opens the Psalter by presenting a picture of the sage king who meditates on the Torah (Deut 17). Psalm 2 describes how God would set his king over the kings of the earth. Wisdom is exemplified in submitting to him.

Psalm 2 was recounted on the coronation day of the Israelite king. Though Israel's kings were opposed by the nations, God himself installed his king. According to the New Testament, Jesus fulfilled this psalm in his resurrection and ascent. The psalm falls into three parts. David describes the rebellion of the kings of the earth (2:1-3), then the Lord's response (2:4-9), and finally the Lord summons submission to his king (2:10-12).

For our purposes, the center of the psalm, where the Lord installs his king, is the most pertinent point. In retort to the coup d'état of the kings of the earth, the Lord laughs and speaks to them in his wrath and says:

> As for me, I have set my King
>   on Zion, my holy hill.
> I will tell of the decree:
> The LORD said to me, "You are my Son;
>   today I have begotten you.
> Ask of me, and I will make the nations your heritage,
>   and the ends of the earth your possession.
> You shall break them with a rod of iron
>   and dash them in pieces like a potter's vessel."
>   (Ps 2:6-9 ESV)

The Lord installed a king in response to rebellion. Notably, upward spatial movement and sitting are the primary metaphors. God said he had fixed his king on Zion—his hill. Zion was another name for Jerusalem. Though the kings of the earth raged, God had already accomplished what they opposed. In its historical setting, this referred to the installation of the Israelite king. But the text points forward to the true king who was coming, and God would install him on the true Zion—the heavens.

If 2:6 gives the viewpoint of the one who grants kingship, then 2:7 portrays the perspective of the one who receives the kingship. The Lord said to the king, "You are my Son; today I have begotten you." God installed the king, and the king heard his appointment. He could ask for the nations; he would break them because God the Father had granted him authority.

Psalm 2 allows us to overhear the words of the Father to the Son when he came into heaven. It offers a heavenly perspective of what happened to Jesus when he went to the Father.[4] It foreshadows the ascension, where God laughed at the kings of the earth as he installed Jesus in the highest throne and told Jesus he would sit on the throne forever. While kings were installed in Israel, the New Testament authors rightly argued this psalm refers ultimately and finally to Christ in his resurrection and ascension (Acts 13:33; Heb 1:5; 5:5). Jesus is God's Son, his representative who went to earth. Now he has returned to heaven and been crowned as the King of kings.

PSALM 110 AND THE ASCENT OF THE KING

A second text also provides a heavenly perspective of the ascent. Psalm 110:1, the most-quoted Old Testament verse in the New Testament, concerns the event immediately after the ascension. The Lord God told David's Lord (Jesus) he was to sit at the right hand of the throne until his enemies became his footstool.

To *sit* at the right hand of the Father indicates completeness. The author to the Hebrews notes the exclusive nature of this appointment: To which of the angels did God ever say, "Sit at my right hand" (Heb 1:13)? Christ accomplished all he needed to on the earth. He died and was raised from the dead, and now he will sit at the right hand until the Father decides the time of consummation has come. Sitting means his work is done, but

---

4. Paul's speech in Acts 13:32–35 associated the timing of this action with the resurrection. Luke again correlates the resurrection and ascension.

not that he is inactive. Rather, he sits as one who has conquered and will continue to exercise this rule.

The seated nature of David's Lord is not the only significant detail; the location is also significant. David's Lord sits *at the right hand* of God—the place of highest rank. It is a position of power by nature of proximity. To be at the right hand is to be as close as possible to someone. Even today we speak of someone's right-hand man or woman. Christ alone rose to this height because he descended and conquered. He was due the fruit of his victory, and therefore God told him he could rule with him in the place of authority. David's Lord will rule over all creation after he has ascended to God's place.

Though the coronation and enthronement of the king was an important day, it was not the last day. For Jesus will sit at the right hand *until all his enemies become his footstool.* An interim period exists—a time of waiting. Kings were called to vanquish their enemies and provide for their people. Jesus reigns at the right hand of the Father, but a time is coming when he will reign in completeness.

Christ did not ascend to float around in space, nor did his departure from the disciples mean the end of his kingship. He went to the Father as the chosen king. His ascent to the Father was God setting his king on his holy hill and God declaring this is his Son (Ps 2:6–7). Again, like in Psalm 2, readers now hear the words of the Father to the Son when he ascended. God declared Jesus has the right to sit at his right hand until all comes to consummation (Ps 110:1).

DANIEL 7 AND THE ASCENT OF THE SON OF MAN

A final important text, Daniel 7, fills out even more details of what happened to Christ when he ascended. Daniel resided in exile in Babylon, and he was granted visions of what was to come. In the midst of a vision, he saw kingdoms rising up all around him, described as uncharacteristic and unsightly beasts. The beasts represented kings and kingdoms that descended into chaos. But amid the pandemonium sat the serene Ancient of Days.

As I kept watching,
> thrones were set in place,
> and the Ancient of Days took his seat.
> His clothing was white like snow,
> and the hair of his head like whitest wool.
> His throne was flaming fire;
> its wheels were blazing fire. (Dan 7:9 csb)

Then, climatically, Daniel saw someone ascending from the disorder to the right hand of the Ancient of Days.

I continued watching in the night visions,
> and suddenly one like a son of man
> *was coming with the clouds of heaven.*
> He approached the Ancient of Days
> and was escorted before him.
> He was given dominion,
> and glory, and a kingdom;
> so that those of every people,
> nation, and language
> should serve him.
> His dominion is an everlasting dominion
> that will not pass away,
> and his kingdom is one
> that will not be destroyed. (Dan 7:13–14 csb)

Daniel saw the Son of Man ascending to the Ancient of Days with the clouds of heaven in the melee of the warring, hideous beasts. The Son of Man is described as common, but also uncommon. He was the son of a man, but also one to whom all authority was given from the Ancient of Days. He was coronated as king at his ascent. He sat on a throne that would never be destroyed.

The image in Daniel 7 is one of triumph, of exaltation. The kingdoms of the earth sought the highest throne, but it was only given to the Son of Man. Daniel was granted a kingdom vision of what would come, and this vision was fulfilled in Christ's ascent. When Jesus departed in Acts, a cloud took him out of the disciples' sight (Acts 1:9). While Luke only provides an earthly perspective, the heavenly viewpoint shows how King Jesus was installed as the king in the midst of the broken and chaotic kingdoms of the earth.

From Daniel's perspective, it was not a departure story, but an arrival story.[5] In Acts it is a departure story. The ascent of the Son of Man bequeathed him with dominion, glory, and a kingdom. All nations were now to serve him. His rule will never pass away or be destroyed. The Son of Man ascended and now has received his inheritance. He is the King of kings, the Lord of lords.

THE ASCENSION AND
THE REIGN OF THE LORD

I have argued the Messiah's ascent shifted but also sustained, prolonged, and even extended his position as prophet and priest. The same reality ensued with Christ's kingship. The Old

---

5. Douglas Farrow, *Ascension and Ecclesia: On the Significance of the Doctrine of the Ascension for Ecclesiology and Christian Cosmology* (Grand Rapids: Eerdmans, 1999), 24.

Testament provides the fodder to understand the importance of Christ's ascent from a kingly perspective. Visions, poems, and songs all predicted a time would come when the true king of Israel, David's son, would ascend to the throne. However, in these texts it also becomes clear the ascent of Israel's kings was merely a shadow. The substance was still to come.

At Christ's ascent he fulfilled all these important Old Testament texts. Christ existed as a king on the earth, but not until he went to the Father was Christ installed and exalted as the king of the universe. Three facets of Jesus' kingship shifted at the ascension: Jesus was installed and recognized as king, defeated his enemies, and rules over his church and the world.

INSTALLATION OF KING JESUS

The Messiah's ascent needs better narrative and theological positioning because as Jesus rose to the Father, he was installed and recognized as Lord of all.[6] The ascension and session were the triumph of the king. Certainly, Jesus had authority on the earth: he forgave sins and overpowered the demonic forces. But at his ascent Jesus received power over the whole cosmos and was installed as the king of both heaven and earth. Jesus could say while he was on the earth, "You *will see* the Son of Man seated at the right hand of Power and coming on the clouds of heaven" (Matt 26:64 ESV). This is a future-tense statement, implying a distinction between his authority on earth and his authority

---

6. Rowe says Jesus being "made" Lord (Acts 2:36) is not ontological transformation but an epistemological shift in the perception of the human community. Kavin Rowe, "Acts 2.36 and the Continuity of Lukan Christology," *New Testament Studies* 53, no. 1 (2007): 55. And it is redemptive-historical; for the first time Jesus reigns as both God and man on high (Rom 1:4).

in heaven. The ascension was therefore not only the climax of Jesus' life, but the proclamation of a new beginning.

In Jewish and Greco-Roman literature, ascensions implied a human being was taken away from the human world and transported to the world of the gods. Jesus could have left in a myriad of ways, but he left in a way that mirrored a coronation ceremony. A coronation was a ceremony of crowning, and when Jesus was transported up, he was installed as the Lord of all—the king of the universe.

Jesus said this was the case when the elders of the people, the chief priests, and the scribes came to question him. They asked, "Are you the Messiah?" He said to them, "If I tell you, you will not believe, and if I ask you, you will not answer. But from now on the Son of Man shall be seated at the right hand of the power of God" (Luke 22:67–69 ESV). Yes, Jesus' cross, resurrection, and ascension were all part of his *enthronement*. Yet, as we saw from the Old Testament texts, when Jesus went before the Father in heaven the Father *installed* him as king over the universe: "You are my Son; *today* I have begotten you."

Jesus' ascent therefore confirmed and authorized the incarnate Son's authority. Disappearing into the clouds was only half of the story. He emerged on the other side into heaven as the king to whom all authority has been given. Without the ascent, Jesus' kingship is not complete. That is why Matthew, even though he does not explicitly speak of the ascension, implies it when Jesus said, "All authority in heaven and on earth has been given to me" (Matt 28:18). Jesus could proleptically say what was about to take place. The ascension was Jesus' enthronement, his installation, his induction, his coronation. Without it, Christ's kingly work is unfinished.

CONQUER HIS ENEMIES

When a king was installed, he began his reign. Sometimes we might be prone to think that sitting at the right hand concluded Jesus' kingly work—now he is inactive and waiting. The opposite is the case. Now that he has obtained the throne, the time has come for him to rule in authority.

Part of this rule means defeating his enemies.[7] The biblical worldview includes other created spiritual beings in a panoply of presences. Though God is sovereign over them, the ascent was unique in that God exalted *a human* (even more than a human) above the rest of the spiritual beings. He, and he alone, brought heaven and earth together. God's plan from the beginning was to allow humans to reign with him. When they turned away from this plan under the influence of a dark spiritual being, God's plan was to exalt them through his servant. At the ascension this plan became a reality.

This supernatural battle of who will ascend can be seen in a paired ascension text from Isaiah 14.

How you are fallen from heaven,
    O Day Star, son of Dawn!
How you are cut down to the ground,
    you who laid the nations low!
You said in your heart,
    "I will ascend to heaven;
above the stars of God
    I will set my throne on high;

---

7. The Westminster Larger Catechism concurs, stating, "Christ executes the office of king in ... restraining and overcoming [the church's] enemies, and powerfully ordering all things for his own glory, and their good; and also in taking vengeance on the rest, who know not God and obey not the gospel."

I will sit on the mount of assembly
    in the far reaches of the north;
I will ascend above the heights of the clouds;
    I will make myself like the Most High." (Isa 14:12–14 ESV)

Though in its historical context this text refers to the king of Babylon, it contains a double meaning. The biblical authors always view human actors as under the influence of spiritual beings. Behind the curtain of world events and rulers lie forces unseen. Lucifer (the devil) can also be translated as "Day Star" (Isa 14), and therefore the king of Babylon desired what his teacher and mentor did so long ago.

The devil sought to ascend, to sit on the throne, and to become like God. So do the creatures under his influence. The punishment fit the crime; when the devil sought to ascend, his punishment was descent: God cut him down, and now he can only be the ruler of the power of the air. He drowns in a pool of his own cold blood. This is still remarkable authority, but less than what he desired.

When Jesus ascended, he went to the highest seat in the universe. Though the spiritual beings desired to rule with God, the Father's plan included humans in this sovereignty. At the ascent this became a reality. The division between heaven and earth, which had been made at the fall, was mended in Christ's session.

While we should not deny Christ's conquering work on the cross and in the resurrection, we should also not suppose the ascension event was separate from or has no consequences for Christ's victorious work. In fact, in Christ's session, he was installed over the forces of darkness. If Christ did not raise from the dead *and* ascend into heaven, the whole world would be still under the power of the devil. Though the demonic forces may think they are at the helm, God steers the world to his good purposes through the reign of Christ.

Colossians 2:15 and Ephesians 1:19–23 speak of how Christ disarmed the rulers and authorities and put them to open shame by triumphing over them. While Paul ties this action to the work on the cross, the work of the cross was only a triumph after the resurrection and ascension. Christ truly prevailed over the forces of darkness at his glorification.

At the Messiah's ascent, he was installed as the Lord of all; he took what the devil and all the kings of the earth always wanted. In this sense, he ultimately defeated his enemies in the ascension. He showed them this was the end game. No longer does the throne stand open; now it is occupied. Though Christ conquered the forces of darkness by going to the Father, a time of waiting still endures so that people have time to hear of this new king who reigns with God.

RULE OVER HIS CHURCH AND THE WORLD

By virtue of Christ's session, he has been made "head over all things" (Eph 1:22). He makes fools his footstools and galaxies his rings.[8] When Christ was installed, his kingly work was not finished—in some ways it began. If the last point looked negatively toward how the ascension defeated the powers of darkness, here Christ's rule is viewed positively in terms of his sovereignty over his church and the world.

Though Christ had authority on the earth, only after his resurrection and ascension did he receive "dominion and glory and a kingdom, so that those of every people, nation, and language should serve him" (Dan 7:14 csb). Ancient kings were to rule

---

8. This line comes from the Beautiful Eulogy song "Worthy."

with justice and righteousness, and this is what Christ does. We are prone to think Christ's rule mainly pertains to his work on the earth, but his reign in heaven is actually greater. Jesus is working in heaven. And if he reigns in heaven, then he rules over all, because heaven is the control room for the universe. He rules as the God-Man, as the Davidic king, as the Son of Man and the Son of God.

The first verse of Acts displays the dawning of a new era. Luke begins not so much by emphasizing the work of the apostles or even the Holy Spirit. He places his emphasis on the *continued* work of the risen Lord Jesus. Luke tells Theophilus that in his first book he wrote about what Jesus "began" to do and teach (Acts 1:1). The work of Jesus continues after his ascended state. Acts notes the revolution continues into the church after the life of Jesus.

Jesus began to rule over the earth after his ascent as the God-Man, but he also waits till all his enemies are put under his feet. He governs the world, but his rule is most manifest in his church. It is his state, his assembly, his body politic. At his ascent, Jesus became the head of the church. Ephesians 1:20–22 affirms it was *when* God seated Christ at his right hand that he put all things under his feet and gave him as head over all things to the church.

As The Westminster Larger Catechism puts it, "Christ executes the office of king in ... giving [the church] officers, laws, and censures by which he visibly governs them." Christ governs the church by giving it leaders. Jesus thus exercises his kingship by ruling over his church in a distinctive way after the ascension. As the king of heaven, he now leads and guides his people on the earth through his appointed leaders. According to Matthew 16 and 18, Jesus' authority in heaven is bequeathed to his servants on the earth. Whatever Christ has affirmed in heaven then becomes a reality in the church as it follows his will.

CONCLUSION

At Jesus' ascent, he became the Lord of heaven and earth as the God-Man. Kingship is the centralizing metaphor for the work of Christ. Adam and Eve were made to be the royal family, Israel was meant to be rulers over the world, but they all failed to ascend to God in their task. Christ did what they could not by fulfilling all righteousness. After he had completed his earthly work, one final act needed to be finalized. Jesus needed to be installed as the king and thereby confirmed and vindicated in his work by the Father.

At Christ's ascension, he appeared before the Ancient of Days and was given all dominion. He was set on the holy hill and declared to be God's Son. He was given the right-hand throne and a new name to which every knee will bow. His true reign began at his ascent. Now he rules in a different sense over the powers of darkness because he has been installed to the place they desired. He also became the ruler of the world and church because he sits in the throne room of God as the one exalted far above every king this world has ever seen.

Jesus' Kingly Work	
On Earth	**At His Ascension**
Designated as king	Installed as king
Conquered the forces of darkness	Enthroned above the spiritual beings
Laid the foundation for his church	Became head over the world and church

THE CHURCH AS THE ROYAL FAMILY

As already indicated, Christ's installation as king has implications for the conduct of the church. If Christ is king, then the church is called to be his kingdom—his royal family on the earth. Adam and Eve were christened to rule as sons and daughters, representatives of the true King. Though they failed, Christ has accomplished all.

The church is now coupled to the head, as its body. Israel was called to be a kingdom of priests and a holy nation (Exod 19:6), and Peter affirmed Jews and gentiles together are now a royal priesthood (1 Pet 2:9). Jesus, in Matthew, bequeathed the authority he received on his disciples as they went out into the world (Matt 28:18–20).

Ephesians recounts the implications of Christ's royal ascent for the church. Since Christ has been seated at God's right hand in the heavenly place (1:20) and the church has been seated with him (2:6), then the kingly assembly is to be unified under its king, put on the armor of God, and wait for its king from heaven.

Paul first speaks of the ramifications of being raised with Christ in Ephesians 2:11–22. Since the church is seated with Christ and under one ruler, Jews and gentiles are to have peace among themselves. They are to be an army of one. If one king sits on the throne, then he is all people's peace—no matter what gender, race, or socioeconomic status—for he has broken down the walls of hostility (2:14). Christ has created one new humanity in the place of two and reconciled all people to himself (2:15–16). Through him all humanity has access to the Spirit and is built up into a kingdom and temple.

Harmony and unity therefore are the *reality* and the *goal* now that Jesus has assumed the throne. This is why Paul says we are to speak the truth in love, to grow up in every way into him who is the head, into Christ (Eph 4:15). The church is to come together under his reign of love and spread love to others. Growing up into the head means becoming more like him. The universal presence and lordship of Christ reassembles the church under the banner of love. What broke at the fall in terms of human-to-human relationships mended at the cross, resurrection, *and* ascension. Paul and the rest of the New Testament letters call for unity because there is one faith, one baptism, one Lord.

Second, the church not only unites as an army around its king, but goes out confidently into battle. Because Christ has conquered the spiritual forces of darkness, Christ's assembly is to put on the armor of God and go forth with his strength (Eph 6:10–20). Kings in the ancient world were to fight with their people and be their greatest warriors. Now that Christ has conquered and fought, in his death, resurrection, and ascension the church puts on God's armor and goes forth into battle.

The church is strong in the Lord because it has a great conquering warrior as its king who dealt the decisive blow. The church wrestles not against flesh and blood but against the rulers, authorities, and cosmic powers (Eph 6:12). God has already put them to shame by triumphing over them (Col 2:15). Therefore, the church takes up the armor of God and stands in the midst of battle because it lives in evil days. Christ's kingship is the foundation of the church assembling to combat the forces of darkness.

Finally, Christ's rule is manifest in a suffering and waiting people. Christ's rule does not mean the church is called to go out and rule the world. Christ's kingship does not cancel out the harsh and wretched condition of life for Christ's legion. Christ's kingship is in heaven, and therefore the church's royalty is hidden with him. Christians are to therefore "seek the things that are above, where Christ is, seated at the right hand of God ... for ... your life is hid with Christ in God" (Col 3:1–3). The church is not promised it will "lead a joyous and peaceful life, have rich possessions, be safe from all harm. ... No, our happiness belongs to the heavenly life!"[9]

The church therefore patiently passes through this life "content with one thing: that our King will never leave us destitute, but will provide for our needs until, our warfare ended, we are called to triumph."[10] Christ's triumph is not complete yet; he still has enemies to subdue under his feet. Therefore, the church, as the royal family, lives as appointed to thrones, but also waiting for that glory to be realized.

CONCLUSION

Christ's kingship was not complete until he rose and went before the Father in heaven. Farrow writes, "The unifying climax of the whole [kingly] story is contained in the ascension."[11] When Jesus left the disciples in Luke's literature, both Jesus' resurrection and ascension spurred them to share the good news: Jesus is Lord.

Jesus' lordship is therefore confirmed at the ascension, but it also endures. He did not get taken by a cloud to go rest in heaven because his work was finished. Sitting implies he is sovereign over all disturbance and opposition.[12] Swete writes,

> When He sat down at the right hand of power, it was not for a brief cessation from warfare, but for an age-long conflict with the powers of evil. "Sitting" is not always a posture of rest. Some of the hardest work of life is done by the monarch seated in his cabinet.[13]

---

9. Calvin, *Institutes* 2.15.4, 498.

10. Calvin, *Institutes* 2.15.4, 499.

11. Farrow, *Ascension and Ecclesia*, 25.

12. H. B. Swete, *The Ascended Christ: A Study in the Earliest Christian Teaching* (London: Macmillan, 1911), 13.

13. Swete, *Ascended Christ*, 14.

His work on the earth was complete for a time, but now he rules from heaven—where God resides. He directs the affairs of the world from this exalted position. As he sits beside the Father, God declares to him, "You are my Son; today I have begotten you" (Ps 2:7 ESV). As the group Beautiful Eulogy lyrically declares:

Lift up your eyes and see the riches of the
all-sufficient King seated on his throne in glory
See his scepter that stretches the expanse of unmeasured
    space
Hear Him who holds all things together declare
"All things are mine without exception."[14]

Christ entered into his appointed rule at the ascent. He took the seat reserved for him, thereby displaying he conquered not only sin and death, but the spiritual forces of darkness. Though Adam had to descend from the mountain of God, Christ was brought up before God because he had done all the Father asked.

If the ascension had not happened, Jesus' royal authority would not have been confirmed. If the ascension had not happened, then Christ would not be in heaven ruling. If the ascension had not happened, the church would not be an entity. If the ascension had not happened, then no human would ever rule with God. If the ascension had not happened, Christ would not have been installed as Lord. Because the ascension happened, Jesus' royal authority is confirmed.

Hold your breath. Jesus is the air to the kingdom.[15]

---

14. This line comes from the Beautiful Eulogy song "Immanuel."
15. This line is adapted from Apashe's song "Majesty."

CHAPTER 5

THE ASCENSION IN THEOLOGY

The resurrection proclaims, "He lives—and that forever";
the Exaltation proclaims, "He reigns—and that forever."
—*Murray Harris*

INTRODUCTION

The book before you has been about *locating* the ascension on
a biblical map. I argued the ascension needs better narrative
positioning. However, the Messiah's ascension needs situating
not only in terms of the narrative, but in relation to other doctrines Christians confess. Precise theological grammar needs
to be employed to correlate Christ's session to other dogmas.
Therefore, in this last chapter, I will briefly examine the ascension in *theological* perspective, specifically asking how it relates
to the Trinity, incarnation, cross, resurrection, and eschatology.

An emphasis on ascent does not necessarily imply a deni-
gration or belittling of these other doctrines. On the contrary, a

healthy emphasis on the ascension lifts them up. None of these doctrines can be separated, though they can be distinguished, and they garner even more clarity and precision as one considers how they intermingle. Relating the ascent to the other events also helps balance overemphases that could creep in as a result of focusing on one at the expense of others.[1]

THE ASCENSION AND THE TRINITY

To speak of the ascension is to speak of the triune God. Like all other Christian doctrines, the session of Christ finds its grounding in the triune nature of God. Jesus is known through his relationships, for identity is always formed in relationship to others. John Meier writes that to "tell the story of Jesus's [ascent] is to tell the story of his relationships."[2] Therefore, to tell the story of the ascension is to tell the story of the triune God. The ascension should therefore be viewed from the perspective of both the unity and triunity of God.

The triune God's singular will from time before time was to *glorify himself* and make his name great. The ascent was an essential event in this design. God made his name great through his representative. The ascension therefore concerns not only Christology. Even though the Son ascended, this was a result of his equality with the Father and made possible by the Spirit's empowering. The Father, Son, and Spirit were all glorified in the ascent.

The triune God glorifies himself in *contesting and defeating the forces of darkness*. The Scriptures present not only a battle on the earth, but a heavenly battle raging behind the scenes. The

---

1. If you think I have overstated things earlier, then hopefully this chapter will balance out some of those statements.

2. John P. Meier, *A Marginal Jew*, vol. 3, *Companions and Competitors* (New York: Doubleday, 2001), 2.

ascent tore a fabric in the universe, allowing sight into the spiritual reality. Humans glimpse beyond the earthly battle to the
heavenly realm, where God the Father has conquered through
his Son and now gives his Spirit to his people to continue in this
battle. The Messiah's ascent therefore shows how God the Father,
God the Son, and God the Spirit achieved victory. The ascension
therefore accomplished the one will of the triune God.

However, while the ascension displayed the one will of God,
it also showcased the diverse economies of the Trinity. Without
the three-in-one God, the ascension could not transpire, for each
had his respective role to play. The Son had to ascend to the
place of the Father. Without the Father, there would have been
no place to ascend to. Jesus sits at the right hand of the Father.

Though the Scriptures do describe the ascension as an act of
both the Father and the Son, the emphasis is placed on the pas-
sive nature of Christ's ascent.[3] The Father exalted Jesus, raised
him up, and seated him. The Father adorned him with a new
name because of his obedience unto death. It is the Father who
installed him on Zion. It is the Father who spoke to him and
told him to sit at his right hand. Jesus entered into his reward
at his ascent (Heb 12:2). Jesus went to God the Father at the will
of God the Father.

The Messiah's ascension also has several implications for
Christ *himself*.[4] The ascension revealed Jesus as the one who has
the right to enter the presence of the Father by his obedience
and sacrifice. Christ achieved the right to go before the Father

---

3. Bavinck notes that the ascension is described in the active as "parting"
(Luke 24:51), "going away" (John 13:3, 33; 14:28; 16:5; 1 Pet 3:22), or ascension (Eph
4:8). Hence it is an act of both the Father and Son. Bavinck, *Reformed Dogmatics,*
ed. John Bolt, trans. John Vriend (Grand Rapids: Baker, 2008), III.8, 445.

4. With respect to Jesus as the eternal Son, the ascension involves no change;
but with respect to Jesus as the God-Man, the ascension does involve change
relative to his human nature.

because of his perfect work and sacrifice. He accomplished all—
everything his Father sent him to do. The ascension also functioned as the beginning of Christ's reward. He endured the cross
for the joy set before him (Heb 12:2). In Psalm 24, the one who
ascends the mountain of the Lord shall receive blessings from
the Lord and righteousness from God (Ps 24:5). At the ascension Christ also entered into the fullness of his reign. He was
seated in the heavenly places and took up the throne as the slain
Lamb. Finally, the ascension means he will be the judge of God's
enemies.[5] In Revelation 19:11–16, the heavens open and Christ
returns on a white horse and covered in blood in order to conquer his enemies.

The ascent must also be viewed from the perspective of
Christ's relationship to the Spirit. Though I argued Christ
becomes present by the Spirit, a distinction still needs to be
made between Christ and the Spirit. Christ cannot be collapsed
into the Spirit, nor the Spirit into Christ. While Paul and John
"can *almost* speak of the Spirit and Christ interchangeably (Rom
8:9–10; John 14:23) ... the two while intimately related neverthe-
less remain distinct," as Orr puts it.[6] The presence of the Spirit
does not override Christ's absence, but the Spirit does mediate
Christ's presence.

The Messiah's ascent thus finds its meaning, coherency, and
significance from the triune God. This God has one will but different economies. When put into this perspective, it becomes
clear Christ's ascent has implications for all three persons of the

---

5. These three angles are taken from Peter Toon, *The Ascension of Our Lord*
(Nashville: Thomas Nelson, 1984), 145–49.

6. Peter Orr, *Exalted above the Heavens: The Risen and Ascended Christ*, New
Studies in Biblical Theology 47 (Downers Grove, IL: IVP Academic, 2019), 61. I
largely follow Orr in his third chapter, where he examines the relationship
between the Spirit and Christ.

Trinity. This is not a solitary christological event. The Son now sits with the Father in heaven, and they both send the Spirit to accomplish their unified will.

THE ASCENSION
AND THE INCARNATION

I have emphasized the ascension as a climactic moment in Christ's work. To some this might seem to be at the expense of other doctrines of Christ's work—particularly the incarnation. However, the ascent launches us back to Christ's work on the earth. The incarnation was not a lesser stage that had to be passed through—the ascension fulfills and completes the goal of the incarnation.[7]

Jesus descended in the flesh and rose in the flesh to redeem flesh. Temporal, material, and physical dimensions are therefore not repudiated in the ascension. In the ascension, they are affirmed.[8] In the Messiah's ascent, flesh is brought up to the spiritual realm, where God resides, showing God will forever dwell with humanity. Jesus exalts human essence and abides in perfect fellowship with God himself.[9] The ascension verifies the incarnation. But how specifically do these two movements relate to each other? In one he descended and in another he ascended. Does the ascension reverse the incarnation? The Scriptures do not present it this way. Rather, descending and ascending are connected—even viewed as one movement.

---

7. Space precludes developing the relationship between Jesus' baptism and transfiguration with his ascent. However, in both the baptism and transfiguration there was an ascent and revelation of Jesus' true glory that foreshadowed the ascent.

8. Douglas Farrow, *Ascension and Ecclesia: On the Significance of the Doctrine of the Ascension for Ecclesiology and Christian Cosmology* (Grand Rapids: Eerdmans, 1999), 47.

9. Karl Barth, *Church Dogmatics* (Edinburgh: T&T Clark, 1932–1967), IV.15.2, 117.

Paul connects these two voyages in Ephesians 4:9–10. "In saying, 'He ascended,' what does it mean but that he had also descended into the lower regions of the earth? He who descended is the one who also ascended far above all the heavens, that he might fill all things." Christ's descent relates to his ascent.[10] Philippians 2:5–11 also affirms this interrelation. Christ emptied himself by becoming a man; therefore God highly exalted him above every name. Christ descended to ascend. These two acts do not cancel each other out; they restore what was broken at the fall. Descent and ascent are a twofold movement in the flesh. In one he came to us in the flesh, and in the other he brought us in the flesh to God.[11] Christ descended in order to bring God to humanity, and he ascended to bring humanity to God.

We cannot conflate the incarnation and the ascension, but we also cannot ultimately separate them. Conflation means their particular nature loses force; estrangement between them cuts the root from the flower but still tries to enjoy the bloom. Both continuity and discontinuity exist between the earthly Jesus and the heavenly Christ.

Giorgio Buccellati writes that in the "incarnation the eternal joined the temporal, so with the Ascension the temporal joined the eternal."[12] Both doctrines are vital in their own respect, but one must follow the other. There is an order and progression. As Barth says, he who goes into the far country does so in order that humanity may return home.[13] What is shocking is this

---

10. Matthew Bates helpfully describes the gospel as a V-shaped story: from exaltation to humiliation to enthronement. Matthew W. Bates, *Salvation by Allegiance Alone: Rethinking Faith, Works, and the Gospel of Jesus the King* (Grand Rapids: Baker Academic, 2017).

11. Farrow, *Ascension and Ecclesia*, 58.

12. Giorgio Buccellati, "Ascension, Parousia, and the Sacred Heart: Structural Correlations," *Communio* 25 (Spring 1998): 87–88.

13. Barth, *Church Dogmatics* IV.15.2, 43.

bequeathing of authority was granted to someone who had no majesty or beauty, but to the despised and crucified Jesus of Nazareth. He ascended as the bloodied, crucified, and scarred Lord.

THE ASCENSION AND THE CROSS

A study of the ascension could fall into the snare of neglecting the cross as well. If the ascent concerns Christ's exaltation, then it would be easy to overlook his shame. Christ's humiliation and exaltation can be bifurcated, with one taking the lead and overshadowing the other. But in the Scriptures humiliation and exaltation come in tandem. The ascension and the cross are intimately related, and to separate them would distort both doctrines. Though the connections between the cross and Christ's session are abundant, I will restrict myself to two here.

First, the ascension (and resurrection) reveals the truth about the cross. Before Christ's session, the reality of the cross was hidden and concealed; now it is exposed. Modern Christians have a difficult time viewing the cross as the followers of Jesus initially did. All of their writings come to us after Christ's ascent, and therefore they speak of the cross differently from how they first felt. Fear, mourning, and confusion filled their hearts when Christ was crucified. Darkness filled not only the sky but their very beings as Christ was nailed to the cross as a criminal. The cross was the greatest tragedy they had ever encountered.

The only reason they could later speak of the cross as central to the good news was because the Father vindicated Christ's work on the cross. Without the resurrection and ascension, Jesus would have gone into world history as "an obscure and unsuccessful Jewish eccentric and revolutionary like so many others"— if he would have gone into history at all.[14] Christ's work on the

---

14. Barth, *Church Dogmatics* IV.15.3, 168.

cross was *hidden* until the glorification of Christ. At Christ's res-
urrection-ascent, the glory of Christ's work on the cross was
revealed. "His exaltation is a real change, a state gained as a
reward of his obedience."[15] The ascension convinced the apostles the cross was good news and part of Christ's exaltation.

Only after the cross did it become clear that Christ's humiliation became his pathway to glory. Humiliation and exaltation
came together, but only once the exaltation was conferred. The
ascension did not rend asunder the cross and the ascent. In his
session, Christ as the forever-humiliated one became exalted.
One must lead to the other. "Christ's lowliness … the scandal of
his suffering … is not merely a fact belonging to the past! It is
the form, the only form his glory takes in a fallen world."[16]

The Messiah's ascent therefore *confirmed* and *revealed* the
truth of Jesus' cross. They must inform each other. "The resurrection and ascension of Jesus Christ are the completed revelation of Jesus Christ which corresponds to his completed work."[17]
What looked like humiliation to Jews and foolishness to Greeks,
God vindicated. This makes Christ's humiliation his victory,
and this is why the cross became central for much of the New
Testament. The ascension lifted the veil on Christ's glorious
cross. It was the event of self-declaration.[18]

Second, the Gospels depict Jesus' journey to the cross as
upward movement and part of Christ's exaltation. Many have
noted how Jesus followed a geographical journey in the Synoptic
Gospels: Jesus traveled toward Jerusalem in the narrative, going
to his death. And he traveled *up* to Jerusalem because Jews

---

15. Bavinck, *Reformed Dogmatics* III.8, 418.

16. Farrow, *Ascension and Ecclesia*, 223.

17. Barth, *Church Dogmatics* IV.15.2, 141.

18. Barth, *Church Dogmatics* IV.15.2, 133.

viewed Jerusalem as the center, the highest point of the world (Ezek 5:5; Isa 19:24). Jerusalem was the hub of the world to which all nations would one day stream (Isa 60:10–14).

Geography in the ancient world was understood as a physical representation of transcendent reality. Mapping things geographically was a visible form of Israel's theology. Christ traveled *up* to Jerusalem to go to God. He went *up* on the cross to be with him, and *up* in his resurrection, and *up* in his ascent. In all of these geographical and spatial movements, Jesus ascended the mountain of the Lord because he was the one with clean hands and a pure heart. Isaiah could therefore speak of Christ's work on the cross as his "lifting up" and his "exaltation" (Isa 52:13). The Gospel of John speaks of the Son of Man being lifted up (John 3:14; 8:28; 12:32), and all the Gospel writers portray Jesus as ascending Golgotha and being raised on the cross (Matt 27:33; Mark 15:22; John 19:17).

While I have spoken of the ascent as Christ's exaltation, the Scriptures view Christ's threefold work (cross, resurrection, and ascension) as all part of his exaltation, but only on the basis and foundation of Christ's current throne. While we can and should distinguish between these acts, they are also united.

THE ASCENSION
AND THE RESURRECTION

Maybe the hardest doctrine to distinguish from the ascension is the resurrection. At the beginning of this book, I noted how the biblical authors sometimes associate the resurrection and the ascension. They slide from Jesus' death to his exaltation, thereby linking the resurrection and ascension (Mark 14:62; Luke 24:26; Phil 2:8–9; 1 Pet 3:21–22). Peter in Acts 5:30–31 states, "The God of our fathers raised Jesus, whom you killed by hanging him on a tree. God exalted him at his right hand as Leader and Savior, to give repentance to Israel and forgiveness of sins." In a real sense, the resurrection and the ascension belong inseparably together, and the ascension was merely a natural outworking of the resurrection.

However, though related, these two events should also be distinguished. In other texts a more precise distinction is made between the events (Acts 2:32–33; Rom 8:34; Eph 1:20; 2:6; Col 3:1; 1 Pet 1:21). When Mary clung to Jesus in his resurrected state, Jesus affirmed he still needed to ascend to the Father (John 20:17). The ascension did not merely temporally extend Christ's resurrected life. His resurrection life now resides in a new location, and that location confirms and validates his life.

While we can affirm that both the resurrection and the ascension uphold Jesus' exaltation, it is better not to equate the two. Luke presents a significant hiatus exists between the two incidents. As Farrow asserts, "To cut short the journey of Jesus by conflating resurrection and ascension ... is to alter the goal of salvation history."[19]

Resurrection refers to Jesus being bodily raised from the dead, while the ascension denotes the movement of Christ's exalted body from earth to heaven. In the resurrection Jesus conquered death; in the ascension Jesus was exalted to the right hand of the Father. Brian Donne writes, "The resurrection means Jesus lives, the ascension asserts he reigns."[20]

These are two distinct but related things. "The resurrection of our Lord was not the completion of His glory. His glorification indeed then began," Milligan says.[21] Karl Barth described the res-

---

19. Farrow, *Ascension and Ecclesia*, 28.

20. Brian Donne, *Christ Ascended: A Study in the Significance of the Ascension of Jesus Christ in the New Testament* (Exeter, UK: Paternoster, 1983), 31.

21. William Milligan, *The Ascension and Heavenly Priesthood of Our Lord* (Eugene, OR: Wipf & Stock, 2006), 1.

urrection and ascension of Jesus as two distinct but inseparable moments in the same event. "The resurrection is to be understood as the *terminus a quo*, its beginning, and the ascension as its *terminus ad quem*, its end."[22]

Murray Harris states the distinction between the two in this way: the resurrection was a necessary prelude to his exaltation. Christians believe Jesus not only lives but reigns, and he will one day return. In the ascent, Christ was granted a position of unparalleled honor that he did not possess in the hiatus between his resurrection and ascension.[23] The resurrection vindicated Jesus' messiahship and sonship, but the exaltation of Jesus made him Lord. "The resurrection proclaims, 'He lives—and that forever'; the Exaltation proclaims, 'He reigns—and that forever.' The two ideas are inseparably but intimately related."[24]

Though Christ's resurrection and ascension are part of the same script, they should also be distinguished. In both of them Christ is lifted up, but the resurrection vindicated Christ's humility, while the ascent was the stamp of approval. The resurrection vindicated Christ, but his ascent confirmed that vindication. The ascension is not an optional appendix, a mere postscript, nor a careless addendum to the resurrection. It is an event in its own right.

THE ASCENSION
AND ESCHATOLOGY

Christ's session not only clarifies and elevates the incarnation, cross, and resurrection, but anticipates Christ's future coming.

---

22. Cited by Thomas F. Torrance, *Space, Time and Resurrection* (Grand Rapids: Eerdmans, 1976), 123.

23. Murray Harris, *Raised Immortal: Resurrection and Immortality in the New Testament* (Grand Rapids: Eerdmans, 1983), 77, 85.

24. Harris, *Raised Immortal*, 85.

Though I have emphasized both the presence of Christ, mediated by the Spirit, and the ascension as the completion or exaltation of Christ's work, his future return equalizes a few imbalances. We cannot conclude that the Spirit's presence is the same as the bodily presence of Jesus, nor that the ascension concluded history. It began the end. The ascension and session were not *the* climax, but the beginning of the climax.

The return of Christ displays the reign of the ascended Christ is not the end. His return is the conclusion. This era has a time limit. Though the Messiah's ascent is essential, it is also temporary, "a parenthesis in God's great scheme of things."[25] He will return to earth to consummate all things. The parousia (coming or presence) therefore should not be seen as merely something forthcoming, but as something to be revealed that is already present.[26] Jesus' lordship is current—hidden in heaven. When he returns, he will make it fully visible to all the earth.

Paul, and the rest of the New Testament, affirm another climax will come. The ascent is merely the front end, while Christ's parousia is the back end. Paul speaks of Christ's return in 1 Corinthians 15 as the finale.

> Then comes the end, when he delivers the kingdom to God the Father after destroying every rule and every authority and power. For he must reign until he has put all his enemies under his feet. The last enemy to be destroyed is death. (1 Cor 15:24–26)

---

25. H. B. Swete, *The Ascended Christ: A Study in the Earliest Christian Teaching* (London: Macmillan, 1911), 32.

26. This is Donne's language in *Christ Ascended*, 52.

That final day has not come yet, but the ascension anticipated it. God will again be all in all, but an interim period exists.
This is the goal to which all history is moving, and the ascension and session are simply the starting point. "The reign of
the ascended Christ is preparatory to the Eternal Reign of God,"
Swete writes.[27]

The return of Christ also indicates Jesus' *real* absence from
the earth. Future coming necessarily implies present absence.
Though we can rejoice in the presence of the Spirit, we still long
for Jesus to return. In Acts 1:9-11, Luke specifically links Christ's
assumption into heaven with his return. The two men in white
robes told the disciples, "This Jesus, who was taken up from you
into heaven, will come in the same way as you saw him go into
heaven" (Acts 1:11). According to the authors of the Bible, the
ascension therefore directs our gaze to Christ's return. It assists
in avoiding an unhealthy obsession with the present and pushes
toward the consummation of history already begun.

Torrance called the time between the ascension and the
parousia the "eschatological reserve in order to leave time for
repentance and belief in the Gospel."[28] As the church cries in
the present, "Come, Lord Jesus!" (Rev 22:20), it confesses belief
in the exaltation of Jesus. To call him to come affirms that not
every eye realizes this, and to call him Lord affirms he already
reigns. We live in the time in between, waiting for him to finish
his work.

When Christ returns from heaven, the biblical authors assert,
two things will happen: Christ will destroy his enemies forever
and restore his people. Revelation provides a graphic picture
of Christ's return and the tragic outcome for his enemies. John

---

27. Swete, *Ascended Christ*, 33.

28. Torrance, *Space, Time and Resurrection*, 59.

describes Christ at the end as the one riding on a white horse (Rev 19:11–16). He is Faithful and True, and his eyes will be like a flame of fire. His robe will be dipped in blood, and his army from heaven will follow him. From his mouth will come a sharp sword, and with it he will strike down the nations. "On his robe and on his thigh he has a name inscribed, King of kings and Lord of lords" (Rev 19:16). Earlier John affirms Christ is "coming with the clouds, and every eye will see him, even those who pierced him, and all the tribes of the earth will wail on account of him" (Rev 1:7).

Yet Christ will also come to gather, protect, and usher his people into their new city. In the ascent, Jesus was our forerunner, who went up and will come and bring others with him (Heb 6:20). The vengeance of Christ on his return is joined to the comfort and relief believers in Christ will receive. When Christ comes from heaven, he will catch his people up with him in the air (1 Thess 4:17). Here they will join him in his ascent. The rapture will be the ascension of believers, where their bodies are transformed to be like Christ's so they can behold God's glory. In the return of the king, he will grant those suffering relief (2 Thess 1:7a), and Jesus will be glorified among his saints (1:10), and they will obtain the glory of the Lord Jesus (2:14). Christ's return means he will democratize and bequeath the glory of the ascension to his people. What happens to the head will happen to the body.

In sum, Jesus' return keeps the church's eyes trained on the future day. It makes us thankful for the present ministry of the Spirit, thankful for the current victory of Christ, but it also keeps us longing for Christ's return. It allows us to see the ascent as the beginning of the end and hopefully keeps us waiting for the full revelation of Jesus' kingship, when he returns to gather his elect and scatter those who have opposed him or his people.

THE ASCENSION
AND THEOLOGICAL GRAMMAR

The ascension therefore needs not only better narrative positioning, but also better theological positioning. To state that the ascension is important is easy, but to state *how* and *in what way* it coincides with other doctrines is more challenging but also more rewarding. When the ascension is correlated with other doctrines, it becomes clear they should be distinguished but that they are all also part of the same script.

The ascension confirmed and continued the incarnation, for Jesus ascended and resides in heaven as the God-Man. In fact, the authors of the New Testament view Christ's descent and ascent as one comprehensive movement. The ascension also revealed what was hidden on the cross and displayed that Christ's humiliation was actually part of Christ's exaltation as he went up on the cross. The ascension and the resurrection should also be correlated, for both vindicated Christ's work on the cross. Finally, Christ's session foreshadows how Christ will return on the last day. Though the ascent was part of the climax, it was not the conclusion.

While these doctrines can all be connected, it would also be a misstep to not distinguish between them. Each of these doctrines is unique in its own right and accomplishes distinctive aspects of Christ's work. The ascent is related to the incarnation, but while God came down to humanity in the incarnation, in the ascent humanity went up to God. The cross was Christ's lifting up and declared his kingship, but he was not installed as king of heaven and earth until his session. In Christ's resurrection he conquered death, but his ascent transferred Jesus' new, victorious body to the heavens. Finally, though Jesus will return in the same way he left, the ascent began his rule in heaven, while his return will establish his rule on earth forever.

CONCLUSION

Christians, even of the low-church tradition, typically follow a portion of the church calendar; Christmas, Good Friday, and Easter are celebrated. Yet Ascension Day is passed by without even a glance. It occurs thirty-nine days after Easter Sunday and is frequently ignored after the Easter celebrations. This overlooking is not intentional, but it does reveal how the ascension is usually viewed—a forgettable event.

However, once one situates the ascension in its rightful place, the importance of Christ's ascent begins to show up all over the Scriptures. I began this book by affirming the ascension can be overlooked. It is an odd event, only narrated in a few verses, and sometimes it is difficult to articulate the ramifications. Because of this we might be prone to speak of Jesus' life, death, and resurrection, but then stop there.

However, the ascension needs better narrative and theological positioning. If we neglect it, we may desert Christ's work *in the present*. If we neglect it, we might spiritualize Christ's current reign. If we neglect it, we might misunderstand the power and mission of the church. If we neglect it, we might forget our call to the world. If we neglect it, we might forget he will return in the same way he left.

Christ's ascension was not an afterthought, nor a superfluous rubber stamp on the truth of the resurrection. It was a unique event in its own right. It confirmed and vindicated Jesus' authority as prophet, priest, and king. However, it did more than this. It not only confirmed Christ's work, but contributed to and even continues Christ's work. Jesus is still alive and directing things from his heavenly throne.

The ascension shifted Christ's threefold work into a new epoch. Before, he was a prophet on the earth; now he is the prophet from heaven who builds his church. Before, he was a priest on the earth; now he is our heavenly priest who intercedes for us in the true tent. Before, he was worshiped as the king of the Jews; now he has been installed as the Lord of heaven and earth, where he now rules from his throne.

Readers should have expected a shift in the Messiah's three-fold office, for the Old Testament presents these offices as incomplete and flawed. They were shadows of the substance to come. Key stories told of a day when an ascent would open the floodgates of the prophetic-priestly-kingly blessings.

Though we might be more prone to contemplate Christ's earthly offices because they receive the bulk of the narration, Christ's ascension pushes readers to consider Jesus' work not only in the past but in the present and future. His actions on the earth informed and directed how to assess his activity in heaven; but in many ways his work in heaven is superior.

The ascension has important overtones not only for Christ's work but also for his church. As Christ ascended, he granted authority, gave gifts to his church, and blessed his people so that they might be prophets, priests, and kings on the earth. The Messiah's ascent in this way offered the church its marching orders. Christians look to their ascended Lord as they battle on the earth. They remember he will return one day to judge the living and the dead.

On that day all God's people will ascend, follow their forerunner, and be with God forever.

SUBJECT & AUTHOR INDEX

SCRIPTURE INDEX

Old Testament